one pot

100 BEST RECIPES

LINDA DOESER

p

This is a Parragon Book
First published in 2003

Parragon
Queen Street House
4 Queen Street
Bath BA1 1HE
United Kingdom

Created and produced by
The Bridgewater Book Company Ltd,
Lewes, East Sussex

Photographer David Jordan
Home Economist Judy Williams
The publishers would like to thank Moulinex for lending the food processor
and Tower Pans for supplying the stainless steel saucepans and frying pans

ISBN: 0–75259-933-X

Printed in China

NOTE

This book uses metric and imperial measurements. Follow the same units
of measurement throughout; do not mix metric and imperial. All spoon
measurements are level: teaspoons are assumed to be 5 ml and tablespoons are
assumed to be 15 ml. Unless otherwise stated, milk is assumed to be full fat, eggs
and individual vegetables such as potatoes are medium, and pepper is freshly
ground black pepper.

The times given for each recipe are an approximate guide only because
the preparation times may differ according to the techniques used by
different people and the cooking times may vary as a result of the type of
oven used. Ovens should be preheated to the specified temperature. If using
a fan-assisted oven, check the manufacturer's instructions for adjusting the time
and temperature. The preparation times include chilling and marinating times,
where appropriate.

The nutritional information provided for each recipe is per serving or per portion.
Optional ingredients, variations or serving suggestions have not been included
in the calculations.

Recipes using raw or very lightly cooked eggs should be avoided
by infants, the elderly, pregnant women, convalescents, and anyone
suffering from an illness.

contents

introduction

With today's hectic lifestyles, it is all too easy to resort to unhealthy and expensive takeaways and convenience foods. For a more economical and healthier alternative that is almost as easy, why not try one-pot meals for parties, Sunday lunches or family suppers? One-pot meals include everything from traditional soups and bakes to international dishes from Persia, Mexico and the Mediterranean and delicious alcoholic desserts – you will find a dish for every occasion.

Preparing food at home can give you a great sense of satisfaction, but it can seem something of a chore, and clearing up afterwards is often very tedious. If you have a busy life, one-pot meals may well be exactly what you need. Cook meals in batches and freeze, then heat in the microwave when you need them and relax for a few minutes. Running a household, holding down a job and feeding the family can be difficult to balance, and one-pot meals are the ideal time-saving solution. They make busy lives easier, make less mess in the kitchen and involve less chopping and peeling than many other dishes.

One-pot dishes also save on washing-up – they eliminate the need for a saucepan, frying pan, casserole and several serving dishes – most one-pot dishes can be served straight from the cooking pot. Try to find an attractive set of casseroles so that you can serve from the pot at the table, even when you have guests. One more advantage of not using serving dishes is that the food is kept piping hot, which saves you the fuss of warming plates in the oven.

Many one-pot meals can be frozen. Make them in large batches and freeze in family or single serving portions, depending on your household. Casseroles and stews are great for cooking in batches: double the ingredients (making sure your pot is big enough), and when the dish is ready, simply leave half to cool and then freeze in a rigid container or freezer bag. Soups will freeze well and can be kept for up to 3 months. To thaw, simply remove from the freezer 12 hours before you require the dish and leave at room temperature, or remove 24 hours before and place in the refrigerator.

the spice of life

One-pot meals need never be boring. The wonderful range of recipes featured here includes traditional stews and casseroles, perfect for winter evenings and large families. There are plenty of meat dishes, such as Irish Stew (see page 53) and Pork & Sausage Bake (see page 68) – hearty favourites guaranteed to fill you up. Fish is also featured, and you could serve Boston Fish Pie (see page 102) for a weekday supper, Cod in Lemon & Parsley (see page 94) for Sunday lunch or Swordfish with Tomatoes & Olives (see page 98) as a main course at a dinner party. There are dishes for vegetarian families or guests, such as Risotto with Four Cheeses (see page 144), which makes a substantial lunch or dinner. Also impressive is Pasta with Garlic & Pine Kernels (see page 149), which would provide a delicious main course for meat-eaters too. Of course, not all one-pot meals have to be wintry casseroles, stews and pies – try Tricolour Pasta Salad (see page 148) as a summery lunch or alfresco meal, or make one of the risottos featured, such as Seafood Risotto (see page 142), for a warm picnic dish.

There are a surprising number of sweet one-pot dishes to serve for dessert. Try a substantial, warming dish to follow a light spring meal – complement Risotto Primavera (see page 145) with Pancake Pieces (see page 167).

A light summer meal eaten alfresco would be perfectly complemented by Forest Fruits Granita (see page 169) or Syllabub (see page 162).

Every cuisine in the world features one-pot dishes, proving how valuable and delicious they are. One-pot cooking preserves many of the nutrients that can disappear during boiling, grilling and roasting. They are usually cooked slowly over a long period of time, allowing the flavours and colours to mingle beautifully. Some of the recipes in this book are well known, such as British Cock-a-Leekie (see page 21), Irish Stew (see page 53), Pot-roast Pork (see page 64) and Flummery (see page 161), for example. Many American favourites are featured too, such as Quick Clam Chowder (see page 25), Brunswick Stew (see page 72), Louisiana Rice (see page 136) and Jambalaya (see page 140). Other dishes are more exotic, but this does not mean that they are harder to cook, and you should not be afraid to experiment with new flavours and ingredients. Try Chinese and south-east Asian methods of cooking, such as Hot & Sour Soup (see page 30) and Sweet & Sour Prawns (see page 110). Visit the other side of the world with Mexican Turkey (see page 90) and Chilli Con Carne (see page 46).

Chicken Cacciatore (see page 79) is a well-known Italian dish, while the Spanish Paella Del Mar (see page 100) is a variation on the classic chicken paella. Try one-pot dishes from Morocco, France, Thailand, Germany and Greece and find out which cuisine suits you – you never know, it may decide where you holiday next!

equipment

Investing in good-quality equipment is important. Poor quality pans and dishes do not cook food evenly, and are difficult to clean. The most important pans for one-pot cooking are casserole dishes, frying pans and saucepans. When making casseroles and pot roasts, you need a dish large enough to give the ingredients room to cook, but not so much room that they dry out.

If you are planning to cook lots of casseroles and stews, a flameproof casserole will be your best buy. A solid, heavy-based casserole can be expensive, but is worth the cost, as meals will be evenly cooked and flavoursome. A cast-iron casserole is best, but remember that they are very heavy when full.

Woks, frying pans and karahis (the Indian version of a wok) are also used for one-pot dishes, especially for stir-frying. Roasting tins are also important for cooking one-pot roasts, with the vegetables sizzling in the juices from the meat. You may prefer a non-stick lining, but whatever type you choose, make sure that it is solid and large, and that the sides are of an adequate height, or you may find that cooking juices drip dangerously over the rim.

You should think about the dishes you plan to cook and, therefore, the type of pan you will find most useful. If you cook on an electric hob with a flat surface, select a wok with a flat base, for example. A thick, solid base is important to allow even distribution of heat. If the manufacturer's instructions tell you to season a pan before use, do so, because this improves the quality of cooking and the pan's lifespan.

You will probably already have most of the other necessary utensils, but there may be some, such as a zester, that you might need to buy. Using a zester is far easier than trying to grate lemon or orange rind and then scrape it from the inside of the grater. They are inexpensive and readily available. Chopping boards are an essential item and will last a long time. Whether you prefer wood or plastic, select a good, solid board that will not slip easily. Remember to use a separate board for raw meat. It is now thought that you should avoid cleaning utensils with anti-bacterial products, as various strains of bacteria can become completely resistant. Hot soapy water is adequate for all pans and utensils; soak them first if there is burnt food on the base.

Measuring jugs and spoons with clear, easy-to-read numbers are essential. Although you can estimate amounts with many casseroles and stews, some dishes require exact measurements. Make sure you have a full set of imperial or metric measuring equipment and remember that the two systems are not interchangeable.

Other tools you will need include a slotted spoon for draining and serving – very valuable in one-pot cooking when you need to remove the meat ahead of the sauce. Try to find a good set of plastic utensils for non-stick surfaces or stainless steel for other dishes – these will last for years. A pestle and mortar is a necessity if you like to use fresh spices, which add a better flavour and colour than ready-ground ones.

Good-quality, sharp knives make life a lot easier, saving time and increasing safety in the kitchen. You should also buy a knife sharpener – using blunt knives is dangerous. A carving knife is ideal for carving pot roasts and other joints of meat. A large chopping knife with a heavy blade is useful for a multitude of purposes, but you may find a range of different knives suits you. A paring knife is smaller and lighter and is perfect for trimming, peeling and chopping small vegetables.

Nowadays, there are ways to speed up preparation times. For a real timesaver, invest in a food processor – a good-quality one will last for a long time. Alternatively, most supermarkets now stock a range of washed, peeled and chopped vegetables, such as carrots, baby sweetcorn, asparagus and salads, as well as canned goods. Canned foods are not so fresh as the ready-prepared varieties and often have little flavour and colour, but some types, such as tomatoes and pulses, are invaluable.

the storecupboard

Although fresh vegetables have a unique flavour and texture, there are alternatives that can make a delicious last-minute supper. Keep your storecupboard well stocked to prevent a last-minute rush to the supermarket. Ingredients in jars or cans will save on preparation time, too – most things can be bought chopped, peeled or flavoured at little or no extra cost. Improvise by using chickpeas when the recipe calls for kidney beans, and for new dishes experiment by using the ingredients buried at the back of the cupboard. Most of us have basics, such as pasta, rice and canned tomatoes, but next time you go shopping, spend some time in the canned food aisle and select a few more unusual ingredients to try.

canned pulses

Most canned pulses are excellent and avoid the lengthy soaking and cooking times needed for dried pulses. Chickpeas can be added to stews and casseroles towards the end of cooking to add substance and a mild, nutty flavour, or nearer the beginning for a richer flavour. Do not stir too much, as they may disintegrate, although they purée well to make a smooth soup or sauce. Experiment with adding chickpeas to your usual stuffing recipes. Dried chickpeas take a long time to prepare and there is not a noticeable difference in taste.

Red kidney beans are familiar to most people, usually from the Mexican Chilli Con Carne (see page 46), and can be added to any stew or casserole. Drain and rinse before adding to your cooking. They make a substantial meal and add an attractive splash of colour. Haricot beans are best known for their use in tomato sauce as baked beans.

Keep a can in the storecupboard and add to anything from salads to stews. Cannellini beans are white, and have a lovely buttery flavour. They make an interesting addition to casseroles and stews, and puréed cannellini beans can be used to thicken and lighten the colour of soups. Flageolet beans are pale green and are not strongly flavoured. They are a good choice for children. Their delicate taste will be overpowered in strongly flavoured dishes such as curries or stews – try them with salads and with subtly flavoured meat dishes.

fish

Canned tuna, salmon, anchovy fillets and sardines can be valuable storecupboard stand-bys. You can base a meal around them, or add them to a vegetable dish for extra flavour and colour. Use canned tuna in rice dishes, salads, pasta dishes and potato bakes. Use anchovies sparingly, as they have a strong, very salty flavour. Sardines are rather oily, but are very good for you and can be served straight from the can with a salad.

flavourings and sauces

Many flavourings used during cooking can also be put in a small dish at the table as a sauce, or drizzled over the dish before serving. Soy sauce is an Asian sauce made from fermented soya beans. Light soy sauce has a saltier, weaker flavour and colour than dark soy sauce – it should be used in a dish that requires no extra colouring. Dark soy sauce has a sweeter flavour, and adds an exotic colour to vegetable, rice and noodle dishes, as well as to meat – it should be used for heavy seasoning. No extra salt should be added to dishes with soy sauce in them.

Tabasco sauce is made in Louisiana. It can be added sparingly to soups and casseroles to add moderate heat, or in larger quantities to make very spicy chilli dishes. Traditional British sauces such as tomato ketchup, brown sauce and Worcestershire sauce can add flavour to casseroles. Add liberally to meat dishes.

Chutney is an ideal storecupboard ingredient. It can be used in obvious ways, such as in cheese sandwiches, but gives a great flavour to casseroles and soups. Try using it as a main ingredient in a stuffing, or add it to a pot roast.

noodles

An Asian alternative to pasta, noodles are healthy, convenient and quick to cook. They store well and keep for a long time. Use in soups and stir-fries, with sesame oil and soy sauce for the best flavour. Egg noodles are inexpensive and come dried, usually in rectangular cakes. Rice noodles, made from rice flour, are just as easy to cook. Cellophane noodles, also known as transparent, glass and bean thread noodles, are made from ground mung beans, and must be soaked before use. Most noodles are of medium thickness, although you may find thicker ones in an Asian supermarket. Long, thin noodles are best for soups and light sauces.

nuts

Most nuts stay fresh for a long time if sealed in an airtight container, although you must use pine kernels relatively quickly, as they have a high fat content and go stale. Try adding pine kernels to salads, stews, ice creams, sundaes and stuffings. They also make a very attractive garnish. Toast before using, as this improves the flavour. Peanuts can be used to garnish many dishes and are great for a satay sauce to go with whatever meat you have in the freezer. They are also useful as a snack for visitors, but bear in mind that nut allergies are common, and peanut allergies can be particularly dangerous.

oils

There are many different types of oil, but plain sunflower oil can be used for most purposes. It is more or less flavourless, so can be used in sweet and savoury dishes. Olive oil can be very expensive. Buy a lower quality oil – virgin or pure – if you intend to use olive oil for everyday cooking. Extra virgin olive oil is considered to be the best quality, and should be reserved for salad dressings and other dishes in which its flavour is intended to play a part.

For Asian cooking, sesame oil is particularly good. It has a strong taste, so use just a few drops for a stir-fry or in rice or noodle dishes for extra flavour. Use only at moderate temperatures, because it burns easily. It is often added at the end of cooking for extra flavour, rather than used as a frying oil.

Flavoured oils such as herb and garlic oils can be timesaving, because you don't have to chop fresh herbs and garlic separately. To make your own, add a few cloves of garlic and/or a handful of chopped, fresh herbs to a bottle of good-quality oil, seal and leave for at least a week to allow the flavours to release and infuse the oil.

olives and capers

Olives are invaluable as a snack, but they can also be incorporated into many dishes. Add them as a garnish or use them as a main ingredient in a dish; try black olives and stuffed green olives, which have different flavours. Both go well with fish, such as canned tuna and salmon. Similarly, capers can add a decorative touch. Add them sparingly to salads, as they have a strong, pickled flavour.

rice

There are many different types of rice. As well as the best known white long- and short-grain rices, you can also buy wild rice, risotto rice (such as arborio) and brown rice. Most dishes can be cooked with more than one type of rice, although some, such as risottos, have to be cooked with a specific type. Black glutinous and wild rice are dark in colour; wild rice is actually an aquatic grass. Red rice, such as Wahani from California and the semi-wild Camargue rice, has a pleasant flavour, and can make simple dishes look spectacular. Arborio, carnaroli and Vialone Nano are all types of round grain risotto rice. They absorb large quantities of liquid and are cooked by a particular method, resulting in the creamy but firm

texture unique to risotto. Brown rice has a nuttier texture than white rice. It takes longer to cook and will not swell as much, so you will need to use more of it.

tomatoes

Peeled, canned plum tomatoes add flavour, colour and substance to almost any meal, and add bulk to soups and sauces. Chopped sun-dried tomatoes preserved in oil are usually sold in jars and make a great stand-by base for sauces and pasta dishes. Add to casseroles and stews for a rich flavour, or to stuffings for colour and for a flavour that penetrates the meat. Use the flavoured oil as a salad dressing and to cook meats, especially chicken.

Tomato purée is very concentrated and you will need to add only a little to your cooking for a strong flavour and colour. Sun-dried tomato purée makes wonderful, flavoursome sauces. It has a darker colour than normal tomato purée and a stronger, more particular flavour, so use sparingly at first. If you use tomato purée regularly, buy a jar and store in the refrigerator.

Passata is an Italian alternative to canned tomatoes. It is made from sieved and puréed tomatoes and is smoother than canned tomatoes. It makes a great base for sauces and soups and can be added to casseroles and stews, with delicious results.

vinegars

It is worth experimenting with vinegars other than plain wine vinegar, as they all have unique flavours. You can make your own flavoured vinegars using the same method as for flavoured oil. Try herb or garlic vinegar – rosemary has a particularly delicious flavour. White wine vinegar can be used for everything from fish and chips to sauces, and is the best choice for salad dressings. Keep tightly sealed to avoid losing any of the flavour. Balsamic vinegar from northern Italy is darker in colour than most vinegars. Best used for salad dressings, balsamic vinegar is sometimes aged for up to 20 years, although you should buy a younger, less expensive vinegar for everyday use. Cider vinegar is made from apples and can make a lovely, summery salad dressing. It has a strong, very acidic flavour, and should be used sparingly.

making the most of one-pot dishes

An easy way to make the most of one-pot dishes is to serve them with a side salad of pasta or rice, or more conventional lettuce, cucumber and tomato. You can change the taste of a whole meal by adding a salad

dressing, either just before you serve, as a garnish, or at the table. Try strongly flavoured salad dressings, such as blue cheese with meat dishes, and lighter dressings such as vinaigrette with chicken and risottos.

Experiment with adding more unusual ingredients to salads, such as fruit, nuts, croûtons or lardons. Segments of orange add a lovely tangy flavour, as well as a splash of colour. Try adding fruit to a salad when serving with meat that traditionally goes well with fruit, such as duck or pork. Pine kernels, especially if they are toasted, make a quick and attractive addition and will not overwhelm the flavour of anything else. Croûtons are often flavoured with garlic and/or herbs and are best added to a salad served with a strongly flavoured dish. Add them just before serving, otherwise they tend to go soggy. If croûtons in your storecupboard go stale, sprinkle them with a little milk, spread out on a baking tray and bake in a preheated oven, 220°C/425°F/Gas Mark 7, for a few minutes, until crispy again – serve immediately. Ready-made lardons and croûtons are available in most supermarkets, and will retain their flavour and crispness as long as they are stored adequately.

Nowadays, many unusual and exotic types of salad leaves are available. Experiment with their different flavours, colours and textures. Try salads made with rocket, oakleaf, radicchio, mizuna and tatsoi, or combine these with more conventional leaves, such as cos, Little Gem and iceberg, and more conventional ingredients, such as tomatoes, radishes and beetroot for colour, and spring onions, shredded cabbage and anchovies for flavour. Baby spinach leaves also make good salads. Look at your storecupboard stand-bys for inspiration – try adding tuna, capers, a drizzle of balsamic vinegar and/or freshly grated Parmesan cheese.

Fresh herbs are a simple and attractive addition to salads. Try adding dill to a potato-based salad or a salad served with fish. A drizzle of olive oil and a handful of fresh, chopped herbs are all that is needed for many salads – chives are an excellent addition.

You can make your own salads of delicatessen quality at home, as well as plain lettuce and tomato salads. Pasta salad and rice salad can be made as a one-pot dish. Add any fresh vegetables that you have in the refrigerator – peppers, diced cucumber, beansprouts, grated carrot – and you can also add hard-boiled eggs, peanuts, sunflower seeds or cubes of cheese. You can make it up as you go along, and this can be one of the most enjoyable ways of preparing a meal. You can use potatoes and pulses as a basis for salads too. Mixed bean salad is delicious made with red kidney beans, cannellini beans and haricot beans, and is quick and easy to make. You can base your salad around any ingredients; try tomato salad with onions or coleslaw with sultanas.

Many salad dressings can easily be made at home and will keep quite well in the refrigerator. Their flavour will be superior to shop-bought versions, and you can eliminate the need for colourings, additives and preservatives. You can add a handful of chopped fresh herbs or other ingredients to a plain mayonnaise to adapt it to the dish you are serving. Try adding a handful of crumbled blue cheese, such as Stilton, to a plain mayonnaise and beat well, to make a strong and delicious accompaniment to stews and casseroles. Add freshly snipped chives or dill for a salad dressing, which will complement chicken, potatoes or fish. You can add anything – try sun-dried tomato or garlic oil in a dressing in place of the plain oil.

Bread is also a great accompaniment to most one-pot dishes, and can be served with or instead of a salad. Slices of basic white bread can be used for mopping up juices from stews, soups and casseroles, but many different and more interesting breads are now available. Most freeze well, and will keep for up to three months in the freezer. Remove and leave at room temperature about 24 hours before serving.

Most supermarkets and some smaller shops now have quite an extensive range of French bread, Italian bread and other more exotic breads. French bread is delicious served with soups, is inexpensive and looks attractive. Serve fresh and warm, if possible, with lots of butter and a side salad. Ciabatta and focaccia are Italian breads, most often baked with herbs. Both of these are ideal for serving with one-pot dishes with a lot of liquid, especially soups and stews. Improvise with the bread that is available in the shops, or bake it at home. Freeze a few different types of bread if your local supermarket has a good selection.

You can make an easy cheat's garlic bread by buying hot, fresh French bread if you live near a baker's. Make some garlic butter using soft, warm butter, a little garlic, herbs, and salt and pepper. Make vertical slits along the length of the bread with a sharp knife, then spread a little of the garlic butter inside the slits. Make sure the bread and butter are warm and that you use only a little garlic – it will taste stronger because it has not been cooked.

A simple way to liven up stews and casseroles and make them more substantial is to top them with bread and cheese. French bread works well, but you can use any bread that can be cut into thick slices. This is a great way to use up stale bread, as it works better than fresh bread. Cut the loaf into thick rounds or slices and spread with a thin layer of butter or olive oil. Thinly slice some cheese – Cheddar, Edam and Gruyère work well – and place some on top of each slice of bread. Towards the end of cooking, place the slices of bread and cheese on top of the casserole so that the bottom of the bread absorbs a little of the sauce and the cheese melts. Depending on your tastes, you may like to try placing a slice of tomato between the bread and cheese before cooking. If you are going to use oil instead of butter, a spray canister of oil ensures that you do not use too much. Alternatively, you could place a slice of bread and cheese in the base of each individual soup bowl before ladling in hot soup.

If you are making a one-pot soup and it looks too weak, try adding pâté to thicken it and add flavour. This works best with strongly flavoured soups, such as tomato, beef and lentil.

To add an attractive garnish to bowls of tomato soup and other dark-coloured soups, place a small spoonful of cream in the centre and run a cocktail stick through it to make a swirl. Soured cream or crème fraîche add a creamy texture and flavour to soups, and should be added towards the end of cooking to heat through.

desserts

Most one-pot desserts are a complete dish and don't need anything added. However, if you have a large family or a very hungry one, you may want to pad out the dish. The easiest thing to add to desserts is canned fruit – try a pineapple ring on top of each portion, or serve with a separate fruit salad. Try using canned mandarin segments, grapefruit or lychees, which go well with ice cream. Fresh

fruit takes a little more preparation, and you have to bear in mind the time of the year – will you be able to get fresh strawberries or blueberries?

Natural yogurt can be added to many desserts with a small bowl of sugar, honey or syrup at the table. Intensely flavoured honeys, such as orange blossom, are particularly delicious and are often attractive colours. Fruit-flavoured yogurts are cheap and quick, and can be added by the spoonful to the dessert or served separately in a bowl at the table.

Single cream is a classic with strawberries, raspberries and other fresh fruits, but for most other desserts, double cream or whipped cream is best. You can buy whipped cream in a spray form, saving time and effort, but this is not nearly as flavoursome or pleasant in texture as freshly whipped double cream. Crème fraîche is an alternative to cream – it is deliciously thick and creamy, and you will probably need only a small tub.

If you have a sweet tooth, try adding syrups or jams to your desserts. If you use a canned fruit for a dessert, reserve the syrup from the can to serve with another dessert the following day. Apricot jam goes well with pastries and pies, while blackcurrant and blueberry jams are delicious with baked dishes, such as muffins or scones. Dessert sauce can be bought in many flavours, such as chocolate, caramel, strawberry and raspberry, and is usually very sweet. Use as an alternative to syrups and jams when you run out – it keeps for ages.

Grate chocolate over a dish while it is still warm – much easier than melting chocolate in a bowl set over a saucepan of hot water. Grated chocolate is also delicious sprinkled over ice cream or cream and fresh fruit.

Ice cream and jelly are traditional children's favourites, but need not be limited to the little ones. Make adult jellies by adding a little alcohol and some fruit and serve with ice cream at an evening meal. To make children's jellies more interesting, add some edible treats at the base of the mould before leaving them to set, though these are not suitable for children under three.

basic recipes

mayonnaise

makes: about 200 ml/7 fl oz
preparation time: 15 minutes

1 egg
3 garlic cloves (optional)
150 ml/5 fl oz flavoured or plain oil
½ tsp cider vinegar
pinch of paprika
salt and pepper

1 Break the egg into a blender or food processor and add the garlic (if using). Process for 30 seconds.

2 Add a little oil, process, add a little more and process. Continue adding the oil until it is all incorporated and the mixture is thick, creamy and pale yellow.

3 Pour the mayonnaise into a bowl and gradually beat in the vinegar. Season with the paprika, salt and pepper.

vegetable stock

makes: about 2 litres/3½ pints
preparation time: 10 minutes
cooking time: 35 minutes

2 tbsp sunflower or corn oil
115 g/4 oz onions, finely chopped
115 g/4 oz leeks, finely chopped
115 g/4 oz carrots, finely chopped
4 celery sticks, finely chopped
85 g/3 oz fennel, finely chopped
85 g/3 oz tomatoes, finely chopped
2.25 litres/4 pints water
1 bouquet garni

1 Heat the oil in a saucepan. Add the onions and leeks and cook over a low heat for 5 minutes or until softened.

2 Add the remaining vegetables, cover and cook for 10 minutes. Add the water and bouquet garni, bring to the boil and simmer for 20 minutes.

3 Sieve, cool and store in the refrigerator. Use immediately or freeze in portions for up to 3 months.

fish stock

makes: about 1.3 litres/2¼ pints
preparation time: 10 minutes
cooking time: 30 minutes

650 g/1 lb 7 oz white fish heads, bones and trimmings, rinsed
1 onion, sliced
2 celery sticks, chopped
1 carrot, sliced
1 bay leaf
4 fresh parsley sprigs
4 black peppercorns
½ lemon, sliced
1.3 litres/2¼ pints water
125 ml/4 fl oz dry white wine

1 Place the fish heads, bones and trimmings in a large saucepan. Add all of the remaining ingredients and bring to the boil, skimming off the foam that rises to the surface.

2 Reduce the heat, partially cover and simmer gently for 25 minutes.

3 Sieve the stock, without pressing down on the contents of the sieve. Cool and store in the refrigerator. Use immediately or freeze in portions for up to 3 months.

chicken stock

makes: about 2.5 litres/4½ pints
preparation time: 10 minutes
cooking time: 3½ hours

1.3 kg/3 lb chicken wings and necks
2 onions, cut into wedges
4 litres/7 pints water
2 carrots, roughly chopped
2 celery sticks, roughly chopped
10 fresh parsley sprigs
4 fresh thyme sprigs
2 bay leaves
10 black peppercorns

1 Place the chicken wings and necks and the onions in a large, heavy-based saucepan and cook over a low heat, stirring frequently, until lightly browned.

2 Add the water and stir thoroughly to scrape off any sediment on the base of the saucepan. Bring to the boil, skimming off any foam that rises to the surface. Add all of the remaining ingredients, partially cover and simmer gently for 3 hours.

3 Sieve, cool and place in the refrigerator. When cold, carefully remove and discard the layer of fat on the surface. Use immediately or freeze in portions for up to 6 months.

beef stock

makes: about 1.7 litres/3 pints
preparation time: 10 minutes
cooking time: 4½ hours

1 kg/2 lb 4 oz beef marrow bones, sawn into 7.5-cm/3-inch pieces
650 g/1 lb 7 oz stewing beef in 1 piece
2.8 litres/5 pints water
4 cloves
2 onions, halved
2 celery sticks, roughly chopped
8 peppercorns
1 bouquet garni

1 Place the bones in the base of a heavy-based saucepan and put the stewing beef on top. Add the water and bring to the boil over a low heat, skimming off any foam that rises to the surface.

2 Press a clove into each onion half and add to the pan with the celery, peppercorns and bouquet garni. Partially cover and simmer very gently for 3 hours. Remove the meat and simmer for 1 hour.

3 Sieve, cool and place in the refrigerator. When cold, carefully remove and discard the layer of fat on the surface. Use immediately or freeze in portions for up to 6 months.

soups

There is something especially appetising about home-made soup, whether it is chunky and hearty, such as Bacon & Lentil Soup (see page 18), or delicate and fragrant, such as Avgolemono (see page 39). Most of the soups in this chapter make a filling first course or, served with some fresh rolls or crusty bread, a light lunch or evening snack.

It is worth making your own stock (see page 13) – and that's only one pot, too – because that way, you can be sure of the quality and flavour. Chicken stock is a good all-round basic, if you don't want to bother making several different types, and it can even be used for fish soups. If you do have to use stock cubes, look for ones with a low salt content and be careful when you season the soup.

The recipes incorporate all kinds of ingredients: an entire chicken supplies both the broth and the meat for two separate courses in the classic Scottish Cock-a-Leekie (see page 21) and a veritable market garden of vegetables is found in Italian Minestrone (see page 28). There are spicy soups from Asia, hearty country soups from France and fabulous fish soups from both America and the Mediterranean. There are familiar family favourites, such as Chicken Soup (see page 20) and some more unusual ideas, such as Sweetcorn, Potato & Cheese Soup (see page 36). All are easy to make and some are surprisingly quick, so you are sure to find one to please you and your family.

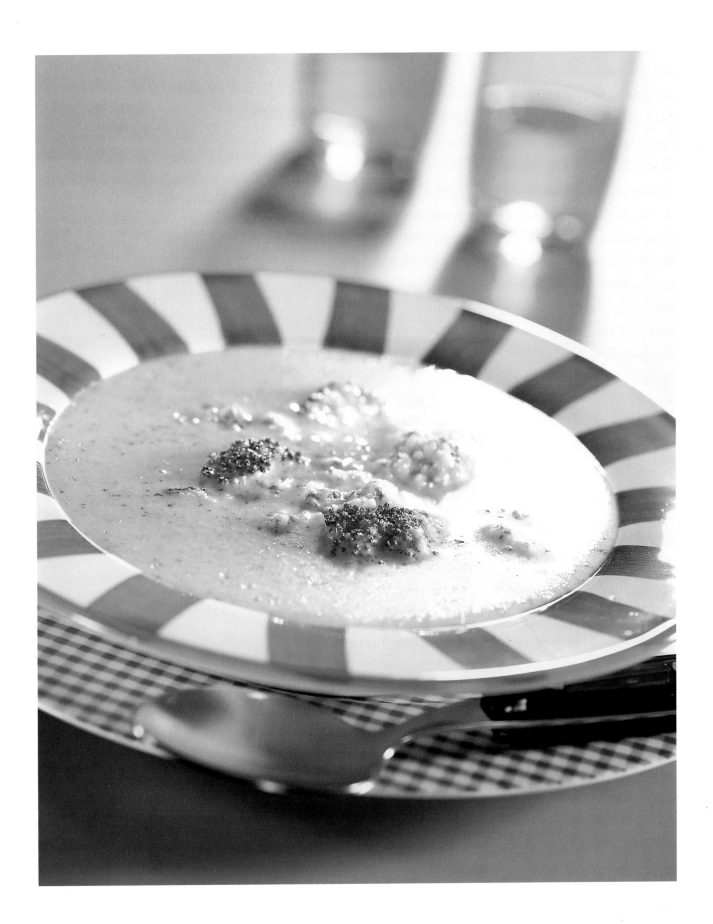

frankfurter & split pea broth

serves 6   **prep: 15 mins** ⟳   **cook: 2 hrs 30 mins** ⟳

Economical, nourishing, filling and packed with flavour – what more could you ask for on a chilly winter's evening?

INGREDIENTS

225 g/8 oz salt belly of pork, cut into cubes

2.5 litres/4½ pints water

500 g/1 lb 2 oz split peas, soaked in enough cold water to cover for 2 hours

4 onions, chopped

2 leeks, chopped

4 carrots, chopped

4 celery sticks, chopped

1 cooking apple, peeled, cored and chopped

1 tbsp muscovado sugar

1 bouquet garni

6 frankfurters, cut into 2.5-cm/1-inch lengths

25 g/1 oz butter

salt and pepper

celery leaves, to garnish

NUTRITIONAL INFORMATION	
Calories	.614
Protein	.32g
Carbohydrate	.69g
Sugars	17g
Fat	.25g
Saturates	.5g

variation

Substitute other favourite vegetables, such as parsnips and peppers, for the carrots and celery, if you prefer.

cook's tip

You can use yellow or green split peas for this soup. The cooking time may vary depending on their freshness – the fresher they are, the quicker they will cook.

1 Put the pork cubes into a large, heavy-based saucepan and add enough cold water to cover. Bring to the boil over a low heat, then drain well. Return the pork to the saucepan and add the water.

2 Drain and rinse the peas, then add them to the saucepan with the onions, leeks, carrots, celery, apple, sugar and bouquet garni. Bring to the boil, skimming off any scum that rises to the surface. Reduce the heat, cover and simmer, stirring occasionally, for 2 hours.

3 Remove and discard the bouquet garni and stir in the frankfurters and butter. Season to taste with salt and pepper and heat through. Ladle into warmed bowls, garnish with celery leaves and serve immediately.

bacon & lentil soup

⏱ **cook: 1 hr 15 mins**   ◔ **prep: 15 mins**   **serves 4**

variation

You can use different root vegetables, such as swede and parsnips instead of the carrots and turnips, if you prefer.

Bacon and lentils have a real affinity – their flavours and textures complement one another. This popular family supper also includes a selection of tasty winter vegetables.

INGREDIENTS

450 g/1 lb thick, rindless smoked bacon rashers, diced	1 large potato, chopped
1 onion, chopped	85 g/3 oz Puy lentils
2 carrots, sliced	1 bouquet garni
2 celery sticks, chopped	1 litre/1¾ pints water or Chicken Stock (see page 13)
1 turnip, chopped	salt and pepper

cook's tip

Do not add any salt until the lentils have finished cooking, otherwise they will toughen, which will impair the texture of the soup.

1 Heat a large, heavy-based saucepan or flameproof casserole. Add the bacon and cook over a medium heat, stirring, for 4–5 minutes, or until the fat runs. Add the chopped onion, carrots, celery, turnip and potato and cook, stirring frequently, for 5 minutes.

2 Add the lentils and bouquet garni and pour in the water. Bring to the boil, reduce the heat and simmer for 1 hour, or until the lentils are tender.

3 Remove and discard the bouquet garni and season the soup to taste with pepper and salt, if necessary. Ladle into warmed soup bowls and serve immediately.

chicken soup

serves 4 **prep: 10 mins** ⟲ **cook: 30 mins** ⟲

A farmhouse classic, this delicious, hearty soup is packed with flavour, and makes a comforting one-pot meal. Serve with a generous side order of fresh, crusty bread.

INGREDIENTS

25 g/1 oz butter

1 small onion, finely chopped

1 leek, thinly sliced

4 skinless, boneless chicken thighs, diced

25 g/1 oz long-grain rice

850 ml/1½ pints Chicken Stock (see page 13)

1 tbsp chopped fresh parsley

salt and pepper

fresh parsley sprigs, to garnish

NUTRITIONAL INFORMATION

Calories 136

Protein 10g

Carbohydrate 7g

Sugars 1g

Fat 8g

Saturates 4g

cook's tip

You can add other vegetables, such as diced carrot, with the onion and leeks in Step 1, or fresh beans or peas just before pouring in the stock in Step 2.

1 Melt the butter in a large, heavy-based saucepan. Add the onion and leek and cook over a low heat, stirring occasionally, for 5 minutes, or until softened. Add the chicken and cook over a medium heat for 2 minutes.

2 Add the rice and cook, stirring constantly, for 1 minute, or until the grains are coated with butter. Pour in the stock, bring to the boil, reduce the heat and simmer for 20 minutes, or until the chicken and rice are tender.

3 Stir in the parsley and season the soup to taste with salt and pepper. Ladle into warmed bowls, garnish with parsley sprigs and serve immediately.

cock-a-leekie

⏱ **cook: 2 hrs 45 mins**   🕐 **prep: 15 mins**   **serves 6**

Two for the price of one – serve the soup separately as a first course and the meat and vegetables as a main course. Alternatively, for a really chunky dish, ladle the whole thing into large soup plates.

NUTRITIONAL INFORMATION	
Calories	.348
Protein	21g
Carbohydrate	.29g
Sugars	28g
Fat	.18g
Saturates	.6g

INGREDIENTS

1.3 kg/3 lb chicken

2.25 litres/4 pints Beef Stock (see page 13)

900 g/2 lb leeks

1 bouquet garni

salt and pepper

450 g/1 lb prunes, stoned and soaked overnight in enough cold water to cover

cook's tip

A bouquet garni usually consists of 3 fresh parsley sprigs, 2 fresh thyme sprigs and a bay leaf, tied together in a bundle.

1 Put the chicken, breast-side down, in a large, heavy-based saucepan or flameproof casserole. Pour in the stock and bring to the boil, skimming off any froth that rises to the surface.

2 Tie half the leeks together in a bundle with kitchen string and thinly slice the remainder. Add the bundle of leeks to the saucepan with the bouquet garni and a pinch of salt, reduce the heat, partially cover and simmer for 2 hours, or until the chicken is tender.

3 Remove and discard the bundle of leeks and bouquet garni. Drain the prunes, add them to the saucepan and simmer for 20 minutes. Season to taste with salt and pepper and add the sliced leeks. Simmer for a further 10 minutes. Slice the chicken, or cut into bite-sized pieces, and serve immediately.

beef & vegetable soup

serves 6 **prep: 20 mins** **cook: 25 mins**

This colourful, spicy soup comes from South-east Asia, where it would be served with plain boiled rice, but it is substantial enough to make a filling meal on its own.

INGREDIENTS

2 tbsp groundnut or sunflower oil

1 large onion, finely chopped

115 g/4 oz fresh lean beef mince

1 garlic clove, finely chopped

2 fresh red chillies, deseeded and finely chopped

1 tbsp ground almonds

1 carrot, grated

1 tsp muscovado sugar

1-cm/½-inch cube shrimp paste (optional)

1 litre/1¾ pints Chicken or Beef Stock (see page 13)

salt

115 g/4 oz cooked peeled prawns

225 g/8 oz fresh spinach, coarse stems removed and leaves shredded

175 g/6 oz baby corn cobs, sliced

1 beef tomato, chopped

2 tbsp lime juice

NUTRITIONAL INFORMATION

Calories 140

Protein 12g

Carbohydrate 8g

Sugars 6g

Fat 7g

Saturates 1g

variation

Replace the prawns with 55 g/2 oz of dried shrimp soaked in hot water for 10 minutes. Add the shrimp and soaking water with the stock in Step 2.

cook's tip

Shrimp paste, also known as blachan and terasi, is available from Chinese food stores. Before use, wrap a cube of it in foil and place in a frying pan over a low heat, turning occasionally, for 5 minutes.

1 Heat the oil in a large, heavy-based saucepan. Add the onion and cook over a low heat, stirring occasionally, for 5 minutes, or until softened. Add the beef and garlic and cook, stirring, until the meat is browned.

2 Add the chillies, ground almonds, grated carrot and sugar. Add the shrimp paste (if using). Pour in the stock and season to taste with salt. Bring the mixture to the boil over a low heat, then simmer for 10 minutes.

3 Stir in the prawns, spinach, corn cobs, tomato and lime juice. Simmer the mixture for a further 2–3 minutes, or until heated through. Ladle into warmed bowls and serve immediately.

quick clam chowder

⏱ **cook: 35 mins**   ⏱ **prep: 10 mins**   **serves 4**

NUTRITIONAL INFORMATION

Calories 356

Protein 24g

Carbohydrate 23g

Sugars 7g

Fat 19g

Saturates 8g

variation

If you like, add 1–2 fresh red chillies, deseeded and sliced to the saucepan in Step 2 and then continue as in the main recipe.

There are many versions of this classic, rich shellfish soup from America. New England chowder uses milk rather than stock and has no tomatoes. This is a version of Manhattan clam chowder.

INGREDIENTS

2 tsp sunflower oil

115 g/4 oz rindless streaky bacon, diced

25 g/1 oz butter

1 onion, chopped

2 celery sticks, chopped

2 potatoes, chopped

salt and pepper

2 leeks, sliced

400 g/14 oz canned chopped tomatoes

3 tbsp chopped fresh parsley

1.2 litres/2 pints Fish Stock (see page 13)

550 g/1 lb 4 oz canned clams, drained and rinsed

cook's tip

Canned clams are available all year round from most large supermarkets. They take the effort out of preparing clam chowder, and make a quick, easy and unusual soup.

1 Heat the oil in a heavy-based saucepan. Add the bacon and cook over a medium heat, stirring, for 5 minutes, or until the fat runs and it begins to crisp. Remove from the saucepan, drain on kitchen paper and reserve.

2 Add the butter to the saucepan and stir to melt. Add the onion, celery and potatoes with a pinch of salt. Cover and cook over a low heat, stirring occasionally, for 10 minutes, or until soft.

3 Stir in the leeks, the tomatoes and their juices and 2 tablespoons of the parsley. Pour in the stock, bring to the boil, reduce the heat and simmer for 10–15 minutes, or until the vegetables are tender. Season to taste with salt and pepper and stir in the clams. Heat the soup through gently for 2–3 minutes, then ladle into a warmed bowls, garnish with the remaining parsley and reserved bacon and serve.

genoese fish soup

serves 4   **prep: 15 mins** ⏲   **cook: 25 mins** ⏲

You can use any firm white fish fillets for this tasty soup. The best way to remove any small bones is to pull them out with tweezers before you begin chopping the flesh.

INGREDIENTS

25 g/1 oz butter

1 onion, chopped

1 garlic clove, finely chopped

55 g/2 oz rindless streaky bacon, diced

2 celery sticks, chopped

400 g/14 oz canned chopped tomatoes

150 ml/5 fl oz dry white wine

300 ml/10 fl oz Fish Stock (see page 13)

4 fresh basil leaves, torn

2 tbsp chopped fresh
flat-leaved parsley

salt and pepper

450 g/1 lb white fish fillets, such as cod
or monkfish, skinned and chopped

115 g/4 oz cooked peeled prawns

NUTRITIONAL INFORMATION

Calories 276

Protein 30g

Carbohydrate 7g

Sugars 5g

Fat 12g

Saturates 6g

---

variation

You could also use haddock, ling or sea bass to make this dish. If you are on a budget, coley would make a cheaper alternative.

---

cook's tip

Monkfish is a good choice for this soup, as it has only a single central bone down the tail. Make sure you peel off the grey membrane from the flesh before chopping and cooking.

1 Melt the butter in a large, heavy-based saucepan. Add the chopped onion and garlic and cook over a low heat, stirring occasionally, for 5 minutes, or until softened.

2 Add the streaky bacon and celery and cook, stirring frequently, for a further 2 minutes.

3 Add the tomatoes and their juices, the wine, stock, basil and 1 tablespoon of the parsley. Season to taste with salt and pepper. Bring to the boil, then reduce the heat and simmer for 10 minutes.

4 Add the fish and cook for 5 minutes, or until the fish is opaque. Add the prawns and heat through gently for 3 minutes. Ladle into a warmed tureen, garnish with the remaining parsley and serve immediately.

minestrone

⏱ **cook: 1 hr 30 mins–2 hrs**   ⏱ **prep: 15 mins**   **serves 4**

variation

Although the haricot beans are a traditional ingredient for this soup, you could substitute cannellini or pinto beans, if you prefer.

Ever-popular, this fabulous Italian soup contains a cornucopia of fresh and dried vegetables – virtually every Italian cook has their own personal version of the recipe.

INGREDIENTS

3 tbsp olive oil

2 onions, chopped

½ small green or Savoy cabbage, thick stalks removed and leaves shredded

2 courgettes, chopped

2 celery sticks, chopped

2 carrots, chopped

2 potatoes, chopped

4 large tomatoes, peeled and chopped

115 g/4 oz dried haricot beans, soaked overnight in enough cold water to cover

1.2 litres/2 pints Chicken or Vegetable Stock (see page 13)

115 g/4 oz dried soup pasta

salt and pepper

freshly shaved Parmesan cheese, to garnish

4 tbsp freshly grated Parmesan cheese, to serve

cook's tip

It is not absolutely necessary to use a flavoured stock for this soup. If you want to make minestrone without making stock, just substitute the same amount of water.

1 Heat the oil in a large heavy-based saucepan. Add the onions and cook over a low heat, stirring occasionally, for 5 minutes, or until softened.

2 Add the cabbage, courgettes, celery, carrots, potatoes and tomatoes to the saucepan, cover and cook, stirring occasionally, for 10 minutes.

3 Drain and rinse the beans, then add to the saucepan. Pour in the stock, bring to the boil, cover and simmer for 1–1½ hours, or until the beans are tender.

4 Add the soup pasta to the saucepan and cook, uncovered, for 8–10 minutes, or until tender but still firm to the bite. Season to taste with salt and pepper and ladle into warmed bowls. Garnish with fresh Parmesan cheese shavings and an extra sprinkling of pepper. Serve, handing the grated Parmesan cheese separately.

hot & sour soup

cook: 10 mins   **prep: 30 mins**   **serves 6**

NUTRITIONAL INFORMATION

Calories 120

Protein 7g

Carbohydrate 17g

Sugars 2g

Fat 3g

Saturates 2g

variation

If you cannot find any Chinese rice wine for this soup, substitute dry sherry, which works almost as well.

In a typically Chinese approach, the flavours of this spicy Eastern soup are perfectly balanced, and are brought together in a harmonious blend of complementary colours and textures.

INGREDIENTS

6 dried Chinese mushrooms

15 g/½ oz cloud ears (see Cook's Tip)

1.5 litres/2¾ pints Chicken Stock (see page 13)

4 tbsp rice wine vinegar

2 tsp chilli sauce

1 tbsp dark soy sauce

1 tbsp Chinese rice wine

1 garlic clove, finely chopped

2 tsp finely chopped fresh root ginger

1 carrot, cut into thin strips

175 g/6 oz canned bamboo shoots, drained, rinsed and cut into thin strips

225 g/8 oz firm tofu (drained weight)

2 tbsp cornflour

3 tbsp water

4 spring onions, thinly sliced diagonally, to garnish

cook's tip

Cloud ears, Chinese fungi that grow on trees, are available from Chinese food stores. They are used in soup, more for texture than flavour. The similar wood ears feature in stir-fries and fish dishes.

1 Place the mushrooms and cloud ears in separate bowls, then add enough boiling water to each bowl to cover. Reserve for 20 minutes to soak. Drain the mushrooms, then remove and discard the stems and thinly slice the caps. Drain and rinse the cloud ears, then cut off any woody parts and thinly slice.

2 Heat the stock in a large saucepan. Add the mushrooms, cloud ears, vinegar, chilli sauce, soy sauce, Chinese rice wine, garlic, ginger, carrot and bamboo shoots. Bring the mixture to the boil.

3 Meanwhile, cut the tofu into thin slices and reserve. Combine the cornflour and water to make a smooth paste. Stir the paste into the boiling soup, reduce the heat and simmer, stirring constantly, for 3 minutes, or until slightly thickened. Stir in the tofu and heat through. Ladle the soup into warmed bowls, garnish with the spring onions and serve immediately.

mulligatawny soup

Redolent of the days of the British Raj, this spicy soup was imported by colonials returning home from India. The sun has long since set on the empire, but this 'pepper water' remains a perennial favourite.

INGREDIENTS

4 tbsp groundnut or sunflower oil	55 g/2 oz red split lentils
2 chicken pieces, about 350 g/12 oz each	850 ml/1½ pints Chicken Stock
1 onion, chopped	(see page 13)
1 carrot, chopped	4 tbsp sultanas
1 turnip, chopped	salt
1 tbsp curry paste	fresh coriander sprigs,
8 black peppercorns, crushed	to garnish
4 cloves	

NUTRITIONAL INFORMATION

Calories	.329
Protein	14g
Carbohydrate	.36g
Sugars	.28g
Fat	.15g
Saturates	.2g

variation

Omit the sultanas. Add 1 cored, sliced cooking apple with the vegetables and 1 tablespoon of desiccated coconut with the spices in Step 2.

cook's tip

Curry paste is made from a mixture of spices, such as turmeric, fenugreek and cumin. It comes in varying levels of spicy heat, so check you have chosen your preferred strength before you purchase.

1 Heat the oil in a large, heavy-based saucepan. Add the chicken and cook over a medium heat, turning frequently, for 10–15 minutes, or until golden brown all over. Transfer the chicken to a plate and reserve.

2 Add the vegetables to the saucepan and cook, stirring occasionally, for 10 minutes, or until just beginning to colour. Stir in the curry paste, peppercorns and cloves and cook, stirring constantly, for 1 minute.

3 Stir in the lentils, pour in the stock and bring to the boil. Return the chicken to the pan with the sultanas, cover and simmer over a low heat for 1¼–1½ hours.

4 Remove the chicken from the saucepan. Remove and discard the skin and cut the flesh into bite-sized pieces. Return them to the saucepan to heat through and season to taste with salt. Ladle the soup into warmed bowls, garnish with fresh coriander sprigs and serve.

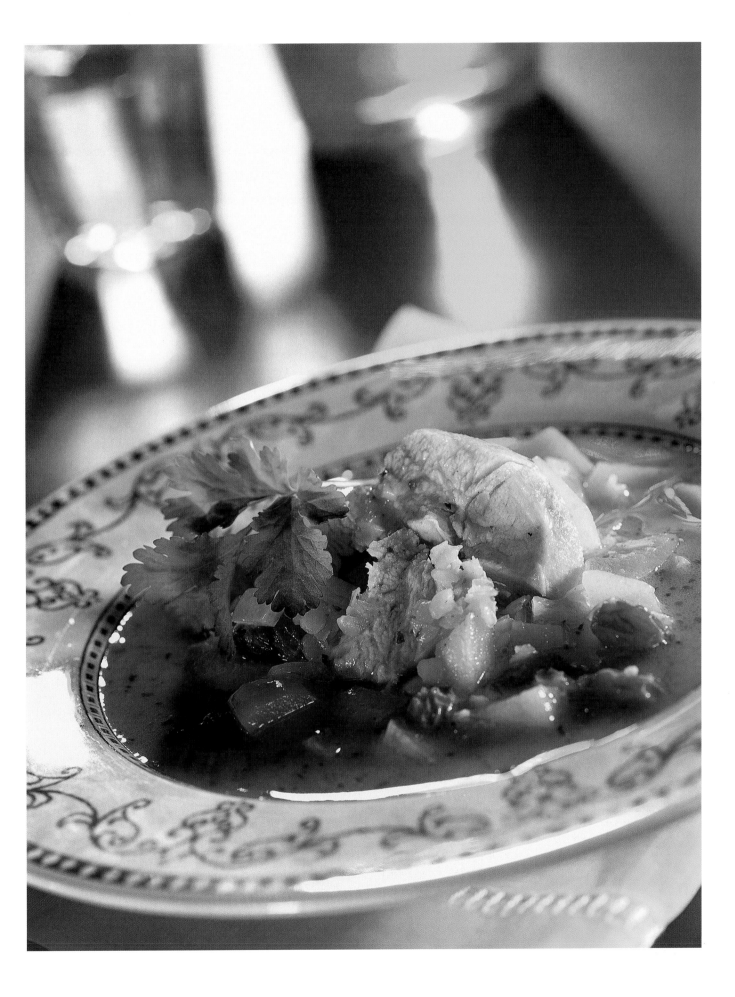

umbrian onion soup

serves 4   prep: 20 mins   cook: 1 hr

Like traditional Genoese Fish Soup (see page 26), this is a substantial and warming country soup which originally comes from northern Italy. Serve it with plenty of fresh, crusty bread.

INGREDIENTS

700 g/1 lb 9 oz onions

115 g/4 oz rindless streaky bacon or pancetta, chopped

25 g/1 oz unsalted butter

2 tbsp olive oil

2 tsp sugar

salt and pepper

1.2 litres/2 pints Chicken Stock (see page 13)

350 g/12 oz plum tomatoes, peeled and chopped

12 fresh basil leaves

freshly grated Parmesan cheese, to serve

NUTRITIONAL INFORMATION

Calories 300

Protein 7g

Carbohydrate 19g

Sugars 15g

Fat 23g

Saturates 9g

1 Thinly slice the onions and reserve. Place the bacon in a large, heavy-based saucepan and cook over a low heat, stirring, for 5 minutes, or until the fat begins to run. Add the butter, olive oil, sliced onions, sugar and a pinch of salt and stir to mix. Cover and cook, stirring occasionally, for 15–20 minutes, or until the onions are golden brown.

2 Pour in the stock, add the tomatoes and season to taste with salt and pepper. Cover and simmer, stirring occasionally, for 30 minutes.

3 Tear 8 of the basil leaves into pieces and stir into the soup, then taste and adjust the seasoning, if necessary. Ladle the soup into warmed bowls, garnish with the remaining basil leaves and serve, handing the Parmesan cheese round separately.

cook's tip

The best onions to use for this soup are sweet white Italian onions. These have a very mild flavour, which complements the other ingredients perfectly.

potato, carrot & leek soup

 cook: 45 mins   prep: 10 mins   serves 4

Once you have tried this thick, rich, substantial soup, it is sure to become a family favourite for its creamy taste and velvety texture. There is also an added bonus – it is easy and inexpensive to make.

NUTRITIONAL INFORMATION

Calories	.317
Protein	5g
Carbohydrate	.31g
Sugars	.9g
Fat	.20g
Saturates	.13g

INGREDIENTS

25 g/1 oz butter

3 potatoes, chopped

3 carrots, chopped

3 leeks, chopped

1.2 litres/2 pints Chicken Stock

(see page 13)

½ tsp sugar

½ tsp freshly grated nutmeg

salt and pepper

3 tbsp double cream, plus extra

to garnish

cook's tip

This soup is also delicious made with leftover stock from boiling a side of bacon or gammon, or made with Beef Stock (see page 13).

1 Melt the butter in a large, heavy-based saucepan. Add the potatoes, carrots and leeks and cook over a low heat, stirring occasionally, for 10 minutes.

2 Pour in the stock and bring to the boil. Reduce the heat, partially cover the saucepan and simmer for 30 minutes, or until

the vegetables are tender. Remove from the heat and leave to cool slightly.

3 Pour the mixture into a blender or food processor and process until smooth. Return the soup to the rinsed-out saucepan, then stir in the sugar and nutmeg and season to taste with salt and pepper. Return to the heat

and stir in the cream. Ladle the soup into warmed bowls and serve immediately, garnished with a swirl of cream on top.

sweetcorn, potato & cheese soup

 cook: 12–15 mins   prep: 20 mins   serves 4

NUTRITIONAL INFORMATION

Calories 860

Protein 16g

Carbohydrate 54g

Sugars 15g

Fat 66g

Saturates 41g

variation

If you can't find fresh sage, substitute a pinch of dried sage for the chopped leaves in Step 3 and omit the garnish.

This easy-to-make, satisfying soup is put together with mainly storecupboard ingredients. It is the perfect choice for a Sunday brunch, as it takes very little effort or concentration.

INGREDIENTS

25 g/1 oz butter

2 shallots, finely chopped

225 g/8 oz potatoes, diced

4 tbsp plain flour

2 tbsp dry white wine

300 ml/10 fl oz milk

325 g/11½ oz canned sweetcorn, drained

85 g/3 oz Gruyère, Emmenthal or Cheddar cheese, grated

8–10 fresh sage leaves, chopped

425 ml/15 fl oz double cream

fresh sage sprigs, to garnish

CROUTONS

2–3 slices of day-old white bread

2 tbsp olive oil

cook's tip

When you are cooking croûtons, make sure the oil is very hot before adding the bread cubes, otherwise the cubes may turn out soggy rather than crisp.

1 To make the croûtons, cut the crusts off the bread slices, then cut the remaining bread into 5-mm/ ¼-inch squares. Heat the olive oil in a heavy-based frying pan and add the bread cubes. Cook, tossing and stirring constantly, until evenly coloured. Drain the croûtons thoroughly on kitchen paper and reserve.

2 Melt the butter in a large, heavy-based saucepan. Add the shallots and cook over a low heat, stirring occasionally, for 5 minutes, or until softened. Add the potatoes and cook, stirring, for 2 minutes.

3 Sprinkle in the flour and cook, stirring, for 1 minute. Remove the saucepan from the heat and stir in the white wine, then gradually stir in the milk. Return the saucepan to the heat and bring to the boil stirring constantly, then reduce the heat and simmer.

4 Stir in the sweetcorn kernels, grated cheese, chopped sage and cream and heat through gently until the cheese has just melted. Ladle the soup into warmed bowls, scatter over the croûtons, garnish with fresh sage sprigs and serve immediately.

broccoli & stilton soup

serves 4   **prep: 15 mins**   **cook: 30 mins**

This soup looks pretty, smells wonderful and tastes absolutely fabulous – just the thing for a midweek supper, or you could serve it with crackers and cheese for a filling weekend lunch.

INGREDIENTS

25 g/1 oz butter

1 leek, chopped

1 onion, chopped

350 g/12 oz broccoli, cut into florets

1 potato, chopped

600 ml/1 pint Chicken Stock
(see page 13)

300 ml/10 fl oz milk

3 tbsp double cream

salt and pepper

140 g/5 oz Stilton cheese, crumbled

NUTRITIONAL INFORMATION

Calories	.407
Protein	.16g
Carbohydrate	.17g
Sugars	.9g
Fat	.31g
Saturates	.19g

cook's tip

Be careful not to add too much salt when seasoning the soup in Step 3 – the crumbled Stilton is likely to have made it quite salty already.

1 Melt the butter in a large saucepan. Add the leek and onion and cook over a low heat, stirring, for 5 minutes, or until softened. Reserve 2–3 broccoli florets for the garnish and stir in the remainder with the potato.

2 Pour in the stock, bring to the boil, then cover and simmer for 20 minutes, or

until the vegetables are tender. Remove from the heat and leave to cool slightly. Pour the mixture into a blender or food processor and process to a smooth purée. Push the purée through a sieve with a wooden spoon into the rinsed-out pan.

3 Add the milk and cream and season to taste with salt and pepper. Re-heat

the soup gently. Meanwhile, blanch the reserved broccoli florets in boiling water for 30 seconds. Drain and refresh under cold running water, then slice thinly. When the soup is hot, stir in the cheese until it has just melted. Ladle the soup into warmed bowls, garnish with the broccoli florets and serve immediately.

avgolemono

🕙 **cook: 25–30 mins**　　　🕐 **prep: 15 mins**　　　**serves 4**

*The trick with this simple, classic Greek soup is not to let it boil
once you have added the eggs, otherwise they will curdle into an
unpalatable mess in the saucepan and spoil the texture of the soup.*

NUTRITIONAL INFORMATION

Calories 87

Protein 4g

Carbohydrate 12g

Sugars 0g

Fat 3g

Saturates 1g

INGREDIENTS

1.2 litres/2 pints Chicken Stock

(see page 13)

1 tbsp finely grated lemon rind

1 fresh thyme sprig

1 fresh parsley sprig

55 g/2 oz long-grain rice

salt and pepper

2 eggs

2 tbsp lemon juice

fresh thyme sprigs, to garnish

1 Pour the stock into a large saucepan, add the lemon rind, thyme and parsley and bring to the boil.

2 Add the rice, and season. Return to the boil, reduce the heat and simmer for 15–20 minutes, or until the rice is tender. Remove the saucepan from the heat and leave to cool slightly.

3 Beat the eggs with the lemon juice. Whisk in a ladleful of the hot, but not boiling stock. Whisk the egg and stock mixture into the saucepan and simmer over a very low heat, whisking constantly, until thickened. Do not let the soup boil. Taste and adjust the seasoning, if necessary. Remove and discard the thyme and parsley sprigs,

then ladle the soup into warmed bowls. Garnish with fresh thyme sprigs and serve immediately.

cook's tip

This soup is sometimes served as a sauce with meatballs. To make avgolemono for this purpose, you should omit the rice in Step 2.

meat & poultry

This chapter is packed with main-course recipes that are sure to tempt your appetite and set your taste buds tingling. There are rich, hearty stews, such as Daube of Beef (see page 44) and Louisiana Chicken (see page 80); traditional and classic dishes, such as Irish Stew (see page 53) and Chilli con Carne (see page 46); quick and simple meals, such as Beef Stroganoff (see page 51) and Chicken Cacciatore (see page 79); and exotic combinations, such as Beef with Eggs (see page 50) and Lime & Coconut Lamb (see page 57). Whether your preference is for hot and spicy, rich and luxurious or delicate and subtle flavours, you will be spoiled for choice.

Most of these dishes don't take long to prepare – one of the advantages of one-pot cooking. Some are also cooked quite quickly, while others can be left to their own devices, bubbling gently in the kitchen while you have a well-earned rest and a glass of wine before supper. Remember that most stews and casseroles taste even more flavoursome if they are allowed to cool after cooking and are re-heated the next day – and you still have only one pot to wash up.

This chapter features a wonderful collection of economical, filling and tasty dishes that are ideal for midweek family suppers and Sunday lunches. Equally, you need look no further for some superb suggestions for entertaining in style – whether the sophisticated simplicity of Paprika Pork (see page 67), or the timeless elegance of Coq au Vin (see page 76).

beef in beer with herb dumplings

⏲ **cook: 2 hrs 30 mins**   ⏱ **prep: 25 mins**   **serves 6**

variation

Substitute other root vegetables such as chopped parsnips or turnips for the sliced carrots, if you prefer.

Serve this traditional stew with its topping of satisfying dumplings to counteract even the coldest winter weather.

INGREDIENTS

STEW

2 tbsp sunflower oil

2 large onions, thinly sliced

8 carrots, sliced

4 tbsp plain flour

salt and pepper

1.25 kg/2 lb 12 oz stewing steak, cut into cubes

425 ml/15 fl oz stout

2 tsp muscovado sugar

2 bay leaves

1 tbsp chopped fresh thyme

HERB DUMPLINGS

115 g/4 oz self-raising flour

pinch of salt

55 g/2 oz shredded suet

2 tbsp chopped fresh parsley, plus extra to garnish

about 4 tbsp water

cook's tip

Dumplings can be given a little added spice by mixing in a teaspoon of mustard powder with the flour – a delicious complement to any tasty stew.

1 Preheat the oven to 160°C/325°F/Gas Mark 3. Heat the oil in a flameproof casserole. Add the onions and carrots and cook over a low heat, stirring occasionally, for 5 minutes, or until the onions are softened. Meanwhile, place the flour in a polythene bag and season with salt and pepper. Add the stewing steak to the bag, tie the top and shake well to coat. Do this in batches, if necessary.

2 Remove the vegetables from the casserole with a slotted spoon and reserve. Add the stewing steak to the casserole, in batches, and cook, stirring frequently, until browned all over. Return all the meat and the onions and carrots to the casserole and sprinkle in any remaining seasoned flour. Pour in the stout and add the sugar, bay leaves and thyme. Bring to the boil, cover and transfer to the preheated oven to bake for 1¾ hours.

3 To make the herb dumplings, sift the flour and salt into a bowl. Stir in the suet and parsley and add enough of the water to make a soft dough. Shape into small balls between the palms of your hands. Add to the casserole and return to the oven for 30 minutes. Remove and discard the bay leaves. Serve, sprinkled with chopped parsley.

daube of beef

A daube is a traditional French dish, in which meat was braised in a single piece, usually in wine. Once, it was cooked in a special pot placed over an open fire. Hot charcoal could be placed in the lid, so that the stew was cooked from both ends. Nowadays, an oven is easier and the meat is usually cut into cubes.

INGREDIENTS

350 ml/12 fl oz dry white wine

2 tbsp brandy

1 tbsp white wine vinegar

4 shallots, sliced

4 carrots, sliced

1 garlic clove, finely chopped

6 black peppercorns

4 fresh thyme sprigs

1 fresh rosemary sprig

2 fresh parsley sprigs, plus extra to garnish

1 bay leaf

salt

750 g/1 lb 10 oz beef topside, cut into 2.5-cm/1-inch cubes

2 tbsp olive oil

800 g/1 lb 12 oz canned chopped tomatoes

225 g/8 oz mushrooms, sliced

strip of finely pared orange rind

55 g/2 oz Bayonne ham, cut into strips

12 black olives

NUTRITIONAL INFORMATION

Calories 319

Protein 31g

Carbohydrate 10g

Sugars 9g

Fat 12g

Saturates 4g

variation

Bayonne ham is a dry-cured, smoked ham from the Basses-Pyrénées. If it is not available, substitute Parma ham.

cook's tip

When you add citrus rind to a casserole, it is a good idea to grate or pare it directly into the casserole. If you prepare it too far in advance, it may dry out and lose some of its flavour.

1 Combine the wine, brandy, vinegar, shallots, carrots, garlic, peppercorns, thyme, rosemary, parsley and bay leaf and season to taste with salt. Add the beef, stirring to coat, then cover with clingfilm and leave in the refrigerator to marinate for 8 hours, or overnight.

2 Preheat the oven to 150°C/300°F/Gas Mark 2. Drain the beef, reserving the marinade, and pat dry on kitchen paper. Heat half the oil in a large, flameproof casserole. Add the beef in batches and cook over a medium heat, stirring, for 3–4 minutes, or until browned. Transfer the beef to a plate with a slotted spoon. Brown the remaining beef, adding more oil, if necessary.

3 Return all of the beef to the casserole and add the tomatoes and their juices, mushrooms and orange rind. Sieve the reserved marinade into the casserole. Bring to the boil, cover and cook in the oven for 2½ hours.

4 Remove the casserole from the oven, add the ham and olives and return it to the oven to cook for a further 30 minutes, or until the beef is very tender. Discard the orange rind and serve straight from the casserole, garnished with parsley.

chilli con carne

serves 4   **prep: 15 mins** ⏲   **cook: 30–35 mins** ⏲

This Tex-Mex favourite is often served with rice, but it is just as delicious with tortillas or thick slices of crusty bread. Buy ready-made tortillas and heat them through in a dry frying pan.

INGREDIENTS

2 tbsp sunflower oil

500 g/1 lb 2 oz fresh beef mince

1 large onion, chopped

1 garlic clove, finely chopped

1 green pepper, deseeded and diced

1 tsp chilli powder

800 g/1 lb 12 oz canned chopped tomatoes

800 g/1 lb 12 oz canned red kidney beans, drained and rinsed

450 ml/16 fl oz Beef Stock (see page 13)

salt

handful of fresh coriander sprigs

2 tbsp soured cream, to serve

NUTRITIONAL INFORMATION

Calories	.437
Protein	.41g
Carbohydrate	.43g
Sugars	.16g
Fat	.13g
Saturates	.3g

variation

Substitute 1–2 finely chopped, deseeded fresh chillies for the chilli powder in Step 2. Anaheim (mild) or jalapeño (hot) are classic Tex-Mex varieties.

1 Heat the oil in a large, heavy-based saucepan or flameproof casserole. Add the beef. Cook over a medium heat, stirring frequently, for 5 minutes, or until broken up and browned.

2 Reduce the heat, add the onion, garlic and pepper and cook, stirring frequently, for 10 minutes.

3 Stir in the chilli powder, tomatoes and their juices and kidney beans. Pour in the stock and season with salt. Bring to the boil, reduce the heat and simmer, stirring frequently, for 15–20 minutes, or until the meat is tender.

4 Chop the coriander sprigs, reserving a few for a garnish, and stir into the chilli. Adjust the seasoning, if necessary. Either serve immediately with a splash of soured cream, and coriander sprigs to garnish, or leave to cool, then store in the refrigerator overnight. Re-heating it the next day makes it more flavoursome.

simple savoury mince

 cook: 1 hr   prep: 10 mins   serves 4

It is always worth buying the best-quality minced beef you can afford, as it will be leaner. This is not only healthier, but is also tastier and more economical, as less fat will be released during cooking.

NUTRITIONAL INFORMATION

Calories 286

Protein 26g

Carbohydrate 21g

Sugars 9g

Fat 12g

Saturates 3g

INGREDIENTS

2 tbsp groundnut or sunflower oil

450 g/1 lb fresh beef mince

1 small onion, chopped

½ green pepper, deseeded and chopped

325 g/11½ oz canned sweetcorn kernels, drained

200 g/7 oz canned tomatoes

2 tsp chopped fresh thyme

300 ml/10 fl oz Beef Stock (see page 13) or 1 beef stock cube dissolved in 300 ml/10 fl oz boiling water

salt and pepper

fresh thyme sprigs, to garnish

cook's tip

You could serve this dish with plain boiled rice, but if you don't want to bother with a second pot, serve with crusty rolls and a green salad.

1 Heat the oil in a heavy-based saucepan. Add the beef. Cook over a medium heat, stirring, for 5 minutes, or until broken up and browned. Drain off any excess fat.

2 Add the onion, pepper, sweetcorn, tomatoes and their juices and chopped thyme. Pour in the stock and bring the mixture to the boil, stirring constantly.

3 Reduce the heat, cover and simmer for 50 minutes. Season to taste with salt and pepper, garnish with fresh thyme sprigs and serve immediately.

stifado

cook: 2 hrs 15 mins   **prep: 15 mins**   serves 6

variation

If you want to prepare this stew quickly, without making a stock, substitute water for the beef stock.

This wonderful traditional Greek stew is cooked very slowly with the result that the beef almost melts in the mouth and all the flavours mingle in a rich, thick, delicious gravy.

INGREDIENTS

450 g/1 lb tomatoes, peeled

150 ml/5 fl oz Beef Stock (see page 13)

2 tbsp olive oil

450 g/1 lb shallots, peeled

2 garlic cloves, finely chopped

700 g/1 lb 9 oz stewing steak, cut into 2.5-cm/1-inch cubes

1 fresh rosemary sprig

1 bay leaf

2 tbsp red wine vinegar

salt and pepper

450 g/1 lb potatoes, quartered

cook's tip

Fresh, uncooked rosemary sprigs and bay leaves would make an attractive garnish for this dish, but remember to remove them before eating.

1 Place the tomatoes in a blender or food processor, add the stock and process to a purée. Alternatively, push them through a sieve into a bowl with the back of a wooden spoon and mix with the stock.

2 Heat the oil in a large, heavy-based saucepan or flameproof casserole. Add the shallots and garlic and cook over a low heat, stirring occasionally, for 8 minutes, or until golden. Transfer to a plate with a slotted spoon. Add the steak to the saucepan and cook, stirring frequently, for 5–8 minutes, or until browned.

3 Return the shallots and garlic to the saucepan, add the tomato mixture, herbs and vinegar and season to taste with salt and pepper. Cover and simmer gently for 1½ hours. Add the potatoes, re-cover and simmer for a further 30 minutes. Remove and discard the rosemary and bay leaf and serve.

beef with eggs

serves 4   **prep: 10 mins** ↺   **cook: 10–15 mins** ⏱

This delicacy comes from Thailand, although similar recipes exist in the cuisines of other Asian countries. Only one saucepan is used, although the dish is cooked in individual ramekins.

INGREDIENTS

115 g/4 oz sirloin steak,
finely chopped

1 tsp grated fresh root ginger

1 tbsp Thai fish sauce

pepper

3 eggs

125 ml/4 fl oz Chicken Stock
(see page 13)

3 spring onions, finely chopped

4 whole spring onions, to garnish

NUTRITIONAL INFORMATION

Calories	.124
Protein	.12g
Carbohydrate	.1g
Sugars	.0g
Fat	.8g
Saturates	.2g

cook's tip

If you are going to serve this dish as a starter, this quantity is enough for 6 people. If you don't have time to make a stock, use water instead.

1 Combine the steak, ginger and Thai fish sauce in a bowl and season to taste with pepper.

2 Beat the eggs with the stock in another bowl. Stir the egg mixture into the steak mixture and add the spring onions. Whisk well to blend thoroughly.

3 Set a steamer over a saucepan of gently simmering water. Pour the steak and egg mixture into 4 ramekins and place them in the steamer. Cover and steam for 10–15 minutes, or until set. Remove from the steamer and leave to cool slightly before serving. Garnish with the whole spring onions.

beef stroganoff

cook: 25 mins

prep: 15 mins, plus 20 mins soaking

serves 4

This traditional Slavic recipe makes a comforting meal on a chilly evening. Thin, delicately cooked beef and a mustard and cream sauce make this straightforward dish taste out-of-the-ordinary.

NUTRITIONAL INFORMATION

Calories	354
Protein	. . . . .20g
Carbohydrate	. . . . .6g
Sugars	. . . . .3g
Fat	. . . . 28g
Saturates	. . . . .14g

INGREDIENTS

15 g/½ oz dried ceps

350 g/12 oz beef fillet

2 tbsp olive oil

115 g/4 oz shallots, sliced

175 g/6 oz chestnut mushrooms

salt and pepper

½ tsp Dijon mustard

5 tbsp double cream

fresh chives, to garnish

freshly cooked pasta, to serve

cook's tip

Ceps, also known as porcini, are widely available from large supermarkets and delicatessens. You could use other dried wild mushrooms instead, if you prefer.

1 Place the dried ceps in a bowl and cover with hot water. Leave to soak for 20 minutes. Meanwhile, cut the beef against the grain into 5-mm/¼-inch thick slices, then into 1-cm/½-inch long strips and reserve.

2 Drain the mushrooms, reserving the soaking liquid, and chop. Sieve the soaking liquid through a fine-mesh sieve or coffee filter and reserve.

3 Heat half the oil in a large frying pan. Add the shallots and cook over a low heat, stirring occasionally, for 5 minutes, or until softened. Add the dried mushrooms, reserved soaking water and whole chestnut mushrooms and cook, stirring frequently, for 10 minutes, or until almost all of the liquid has evaporated, then transfer the mixture to a plate.

4 Heat the remaining oil in the frying pan, add the beef and cook, stirring frequently, for 4 minutes, or until browned all over. You may need to do this in batches. Return the mushroom mixture to the frying pan and season to taste with salt and pepper. Place the mustard and cream in a small bowl and stir to mix, then fold into the mixture. Heat through gently, then serve with freshly cooked pasta, garnished with chives.

lamb with pears

serves 4　　　　**prep: 10 mins** ⟲　　　　**cook: 2 hrs** ⟳

A rich and often quite fatty meat, lamb is usually partnered with sharp fruit, such as redcurrants, or tangy mint to bring out its flavour. This unusual combination is just as delicious.

INGREDIENTS

1 tbsp olive oil

1 kg/2 lb 4 oz best end-of-neck lamb
cutlets, trimmed of visible fat

6 pears, peeled, cored and quartered

1 tsp ground ginger

4 potatoes, diced

4 tbsp dry cider

salt and pepper

450 g/1 lb green beans

2 tbsp snipped fresh chives,
to garnish

NUTRITIONAL INFORMATION

Calories 504

Protein 37g

Carbohydrate 53g

Sugars 27g

Fat 17g

Saturates 7g

cook's tip

Look for pears that are still firm even when ripe, such as Beurre Dumont, Forelle or Williams. Soft pears will begin to disintegrate during the cooking process.

1 Preheat the oven to 160°C/325°F/Gas Mark 3. Heat the olive oil in a flameproof casserole over a medium heat. Add the lamb and cook, turning frequently, for 5–10 minutes, or until browned on all sides.

2 Arrange the pear quarters on top, then sprinkle over the ginger. Cover with the potatoes. Pour in the cider and season to taste with salt and pepper. Cover and cook in the preheated oven for 1¼ hours.

3 Trim the stalk ends of the green beans. Remove the casserole from the oven and add the beans, then re-cover and return to the oven for a further 30 minutes. Taste and adjust the seasoning. Sprinkle with the chives and serve.

irish stew

cook: 2 hrs 30 mins　　　**prep: 10 mins**　　　**serves 4**

Nothing could be simpler, tastier or more economical than this traditional, heart-warming stew. Serve with fresh soda bread for an authentic touch – and to mop up the delicious juices.

NUTRITIONAL INFORMATION

Calories 496

Protein 40g

Carbohydrate 55g

Sugars 16g

Fat 15g

Saturates 6g

INGREDIENTS

4 tbsp plain flour

salt and pepper

1.3 kg/3 lb middle neck of lamb, trimmed of visible fat

3 large onions, chopped

3 carrots, sliced

450 g/1 lb potatoes, quartered

½ tsp dried thyme

850 ml/1½ pints hot Beef Stock (see page 13)

2 tbsp chopped fresh parsley, to garnish

cook's tip

This stew is even more substantial and flavoursome if it is served with Herb Dumplings (see page 43). Add them to the casserole 30 minutes before the end of the cooking time.

1 Preheat the oven to 160°C/325°F/Gas Mark 3. Spread the flour on a plate and season with salt and pepper. Roll the pieces of lamb in the flour to coat, shaking off any excess, and arrange in the base of a casserole.

2 Layer the onions, carrots and potatoes on top of the lamb.

3 Sprinkle in the thyme and pour in the stock, then cover and cook in the preheated oven for 2½ hours. Garnish with the chopped fresh parsley and serve straight from the casserole.

french country casserole

serves 6   **prep: 15 mins**   **cook: 2 hrs 15 mins**

A crispy potato topping covers a dish of succulent, tender lamb, flavoured with mint, leeks and apricots in this traditional rustic casserole – which tastes as good as it looks.

INGREDIENTS

2 tbsp sunflower oil	1 tbsp tomato purée
2 kg/4 lb 8 oz boneless leg of lamb, cut into 2.5-cm/1-inch cubes	1 tbsp sugar
	2 tbsp chopped fresh mint
6 leeks, sliced	115 g/4 oz dried apricots, chopped
1 tbsp plain flour	salt and pepper
150 ml/5 fl oz rosé wine	1 kg/2 lb 4 oz potatoes, sliced
300 ml/10 fl oz Chicken Stock	3 tbsp melted unsalted butter
(see page 13)	fresh mint sprigs, to garnish

NUTRITIONAL INFORMATION

Calories	720
Protein	. . . . .60g
Carbohydrate	. . . . .44g
Sugars	. . . . .15g
Fat	. . . . .33g
Saturates	. . . . .15g

variation

Use a light red wine instead of rosé if you would prefer a slightly heavier flavour in this country casserole.

cook's tip

It is always a good idea to fry off meat to brown it before adding it to a casserole. This will ensure that it has an appetising colour in the finished dish.

1 Preheat the oven to 180°C/350°F/Gas Mark 4. Heat the oil in a large, flameproof casserole. Add the lamb in batches and cook over a medium heat, stirring, for 5–8 minutes, or until browned. Transfer to a plate.

2 Add the sliced leeks to the casserole and cook, stirring occasionally, for 5 minutes, or until softened. Sprinkle in the flour and cook, stirring, for 1 minute. Pour in the wine and stock and bring to the boil, stirring. Stir in the tomato purée, sugar, chopped mint and apricots and season to taste with salt and pepper.

3 Return the lamb to the casserole and stir. Arrange the potato slices on top and brush with the melted butter. Cover and bake in the preheated oven for 1½ hours.

4 Increase the oven temperature to 200°C/400°F/Gas Mark 6, uncover the casserole and bake for a further 30 minutes, or until the potato topping is golden brown. Serve immediately, garnished with fresh mint sprigs.

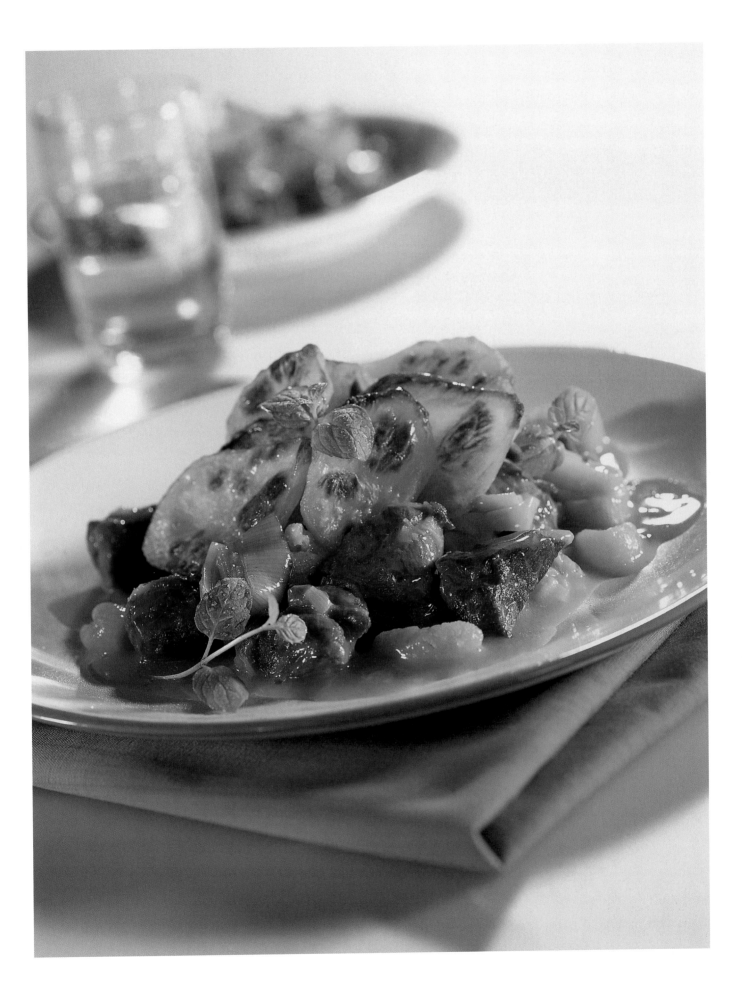

moroccan lamb

serves 4   **prep: 20 mins**   **cook: 1 hrs 30 mins**

Slow-cooking lamb with dried fruit and spices is traditional in North Africa. Stews flavoured with dried fruits, including apricots and prunes, have now become familiar elsewhere.

INGREDIENTS

500 g/1 lb 2 oz boneless leg of lamb

1 tbsp sunflower oil

350 g/12 oz shallots, peeled
but left whole

425 ml/15 fl oz Chicken Stock (see page 13)

1 tbsp clear honey

1 tsp ground cinnamon

½ tsp ground ginger

½ tsp saffron threads, lightly crushed

¼ tsp freshly grated nutmeg

salt and pepper

grated rind and juice of 1 small orange,
plus extra rind to garnish

12 no-soak dried prunes

NUTRITIONAL INFORMATION

Calories	.335
Protein	.28g
Carbohydrate	.26g
Sugars	.24g
Fat	.14g
Saturates	.6g

cook's tip

'No-soak' dried fruit is the same thing as dried, but moist, 'ready-to-eat' fruit, is also now available in bags in most supermarkets.

1 Cut the lamb into large cubes. Heat the oil in a flameproof casserole, add the lamb and cook over a medium heat, stirring, for 3–5 minutes, or until browned. Transfer to a plate. Add the shallots to the casserole and cook over a low heat, stirring occasionally, for 10 minutes, or until golden. Transfer them to a separate plate with a slotted spoon.

2 Pour away any excess fat from the casserole, then add the stock and bring to the boil, stirring constantly and scraping up any sediment from the base. Return the lamb to the casserole and stir in the honey, cinnamon, ginger, saffron and nutmeg. Season to taste with salt and pepper, cover and simmer for 30 minutes.

3 Return the shallots to the casserole and add the orange rind and juice. Re-cover and simmer for a further 30 minutes. Add the prunes and adjust the seasoning, if necessary. Simmer, uncovered, for a further 15 minutes. Garnish with orange rind and serve immediately.

lime & coconut lamb

cook: 10 mins   **prep: 10 mins**   **serves 4**

*This Thai-style curry is so delicious and tastes so authentic that
your family will think you have spent hours preparing it. Only you
will know just how speedy and simple it is.*

NUTRITIONAL INFORMATION

Calories	.273
Protein	.25g
Carbohydrate	.2g
Sugars	.1g
Fat	.19g
Saturates	.5g

INGREDIENTS

450 g/1 lb lamb fillet

55 g/2 oz creamed coconut

300 ml/10 fl oz boiling water

2 tsp groundnut or sunflower oil

1–2 garlic cloves, finely chopped

2 tsp grated fresh root ginger

2 tbsp Thai green curry paste

grated rind and juice of 1 lime

salt and pepper

2 tbsp chopped fresh coriander, plus
extra to garnish

freshly cooked rice, to serve

cook's tip

Good-quality, ready-made
Thai curry pastes are available
in large supermarkets and
specialist Asian food stores,
and add an authentic flavour
to home-cooked Thai dishes.

1 Cut the lamb across
the grain into strips
about 4-cm/1½-inches long.
Combine the creamed coconut
and boiling water in a jug,
stirring well to mix.

2 Heat the oil in a
preheated wok or large
frying pan. Add the lamb,
garlic and ginger and fry over a
high heat for 2–3 minutes. Stir
in the curry paste and coconut
mixture and add the lime rind
and juice. Season to taste with
salt and pepper.

3 Bring the mixture to the
boil, stirring constantly,
then reduce the heat and
simmer for 5 minutes. Stir in
the chopped coriander and
serve with rice, sprinkled with
extra chopped coriander.

rogan josh

serves 6   **prep: 20 mins, plus 8 hrs marinating**   **cook: 1 hr 30 mins– 1 hr 45 mins**

This richly coloured, spicy dish is among the most popular lamb curries from India. It makes a filling family supper when served with a generous helping of spicy naan bread.

INGREDIENTS

225 ml/8 fl oz natural yogurt	4 cardamom pods
3 tbsp lemon juice	1 onion, finely chopped
2.5-cm/1-inch piece fresh	1 fresh green chilli, deseeded and
root ginger, grated	finely chopped
2 garlic cloves, finely chopped	2 tsp ground cumin
salt	2 tsp ground coriander
900 g/2 lb lamb fillet, cut	400 g/14 oz canned chopped tomatoes
into 2.5-cm/1-inch cubes	2 tbsp tomato purée
3 tbsp sunflower oil	150 ml/5 fl oz water
½ tsp cumin seeds	2 bay leaves, plus extra to garnish

NUTRITIONAL INFORMATION

Calories 340

Protein 35g

Carbohydrate 8g

Sugars 7g

Fat 19g

Saturates 7g

variation

Use a red chilli instead of the green chilli if you want the dish to have a slightly sweeter flavour.

cook's tip

When you cook chopped fresh chilli in a hot frying pan, stir frequently, and keep a close eye on it. Small pieces of chilli burn easily, and will quickly turn black if left unattended.

1 Place the yogurt, lemon juice, ginger and half the garlic in a non-metallic dish and mix. Season well with salt. Add the lamb. Mix well, cover with clingfilm and leave in the refrigerator to marinate for 8 hours or overnight.

2 Heat the oil in a large, heavy-based frying pan over a high heat. Add the cumin seeds and cook, stirring constantly, for 1–2 minutes, or until they begin to pop and release their aroma. Add the cardamom pods and cook, stirring constantly, for a further 2 minutes. Add the onion, chilli and remaining garlic and cook, stirring frequently, for 5 minutes, or until the onion is softened. Stir in the ground cumin and coriander.

3 Add the lamb, with the marinade and cook, stirring occasionally, for 5 minutes. Add the tomatoes and their juices, and the tomato purée, water and bay leaves. Bring to the boil, stirring, then reduce the heat, cover and simmer for 1¼–1½ hours, or until cooked through and tender. Garnish with bay leaves and serve.

lamb with mint

cook: 30 mins   **prep: 10 mins**   **serves 4**

NUTRITIONAL INFORMATION

Calories	.245
Protein	.21g
Carbohydrate	.10g
Sugars	.7g
Fat	.14g
Saturates	.4g

variation

If you prefer, use peeled, chopped fresh tomatoes rather than canned tomatoes, but add 1 tablespoon of tomato purée with them in Step 3.

A classic combination popular in many different countries, this recipe is for a mildly spiced Indian dish of minced lamb, mixed with peas. Serve with naan bread or chapatis.

INGREDIENTS

2 tbsp sunflower oil

1 onion, chopped

1 garlic clove, finely chopped

1 tsp grated fresh root ginger

1 tsp ground coriander

½ tsp chilli powder

¼ tsp ground turmeric

pinch of salt

350 g/12 oz fresh lamb mince

200 g/7 oz canned chopped tomatoes

1 tbsp chopped fresh mint

85 g/3 oz fresh or frozen peas

2 carrots, sliced into thin batons

1 fresh green chilli, deseeded and finely chopped

1 tbsp chopped fresh coriander

fresh mint sprigs, to garnish

cook's tip

To ensure that the lamb is lean, buy boneless leg, trim off all of the visible fat and mince it yourself, using a meat mincer or food processor.

1 Heat the oil in a large, heavy-based frying pan or flameproof casserole. Add the onion and cook over a low heat, stirring occasionally, for 10 minutes, or until golden.

2 Meanwhile, place the garlic, ginger, ground coriander, chilli powder, turmeric and salt in a small bowl and mix well. Add the spice mixture to the frying pan and cook, stirring constantly, for 2 minutes. Add the lamb and cook, stirring frequently, for 8–10 minutes, or until it is broken up and browned.

3 Add the tomatoes and their juices, the mint, peas, carrots, chilli and fresh coriander. Cook, stirring constantly, for 3–5 minutes, then serve, garnished with fresh mint sprigs.

five-spice lamb

serves 4   **prep: 15 mins** ⏱   **cook: 12–15 mins** ⏱

Chinese five-spice powder, ginger and soy and hoisin sauces flavour this quick and easy aromatic stir-fry – an unusual, Eastern-style dish, which is a great idea for impressing guests.

NUTRITIONAL INFORMATION

Calories 367

Protein 36g

Carbohydrate 7g

Sugars 5g

Fat 22g

Saturates 8g

INGREDIENTS

650 g/1 lb 7 oz lamb fillet

2 tbsp groundnut or sunflower oil

1 onion, finely chopped

1 garlic clove, finely chopped

1 red pepper, deseeded and thinly sliced

1 yellow pepper, deseeded and thinly sliced

2 tsp grated fresh root ginger

175 g/6 oz green beans, halved

1 tsp Chinese five-spice powder

1 tbsp hoisin sauce

1 tbsp dark soy sauce

4 tbsp Chinese rice wine or dry sherry

GARNISH

2 tbsp chopped fresh coriander

1 tbsp toasted sesame seeds

variation

To add some spiciness, add 1–2 fresh red chillies, deseeded and chopped, with the peppers and ginger in Step 2. Serve this dish with freshly cooked rice or egg noodles.

cook's tip

Chinese five-spice powder and rice wine are available from large supermarkets and Chinese food stores. Note that the Chinese spice is different from Indian five-spice powder.

1 Cut the lamb across the grain into strips about 4-cm/1½-inches long. Heat the oil in a preheated wok or large frying pan. Add the lamb and stir-fry over a high heat for 4 minutes, or until browned all over. Transfer to a plate with a slotted spoon.

2 Add the onion, garlic, peppers and fresh root ginger to the wok and stir-fry for 3–4 minutes. Add the green beans and stir-fry for a further 2 minutes.

3 Return the lamb to the wok, then stir in the Chinese five-spice powder, hoisin sauce, soy sauce and Chinese rice wine. Cook, stirring and tossing the mixture constantly, until the lamb is tender and coated in the sauce. Serve, garnished with chopped coriander and toasted sesame seeds.

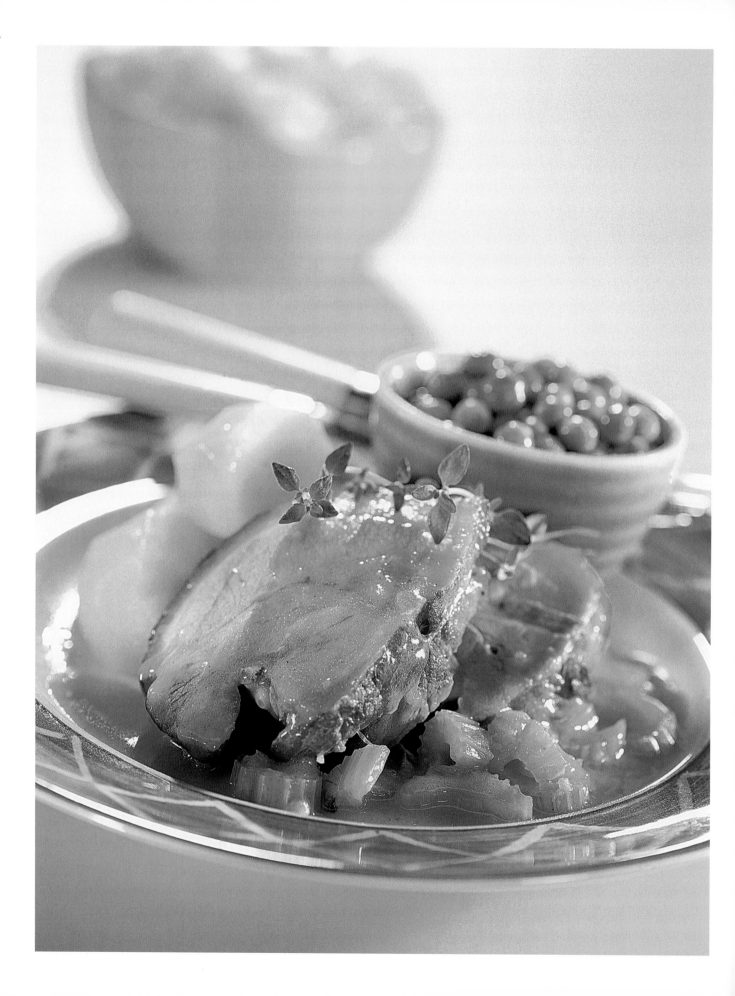

pot-roast pork

cook: 1 hr 30 mins   **prep: 20 mins**   **serves 4**

NUTRITIONAL INFORMATION

Calories 850

Protein 41g

Carbohydrate 12g

Sugars 4g

Fat 70g

Saturates 33g

variation

Substitute 2 thinly sliced fennel bulbs for the chopped celery if you would prefer an aniseed flavour in this dish.

Beef and chicken are the most popular choices for pot-roasting, but a loin of pork works superbly well, too. This is a rich and flavoursome dish that is ideal for entertaining.

INGREDIENTS

1 tbsp sunflower oil	150 ml/5 fl oz dry cider
55 g/2 oz butter	150 ml/5 fl oz Chicken Stock
1 kg/2 lb 4 oz boned and	(see page 13) or water
rolled loin of pork	salt and pepper
4 shallots, chopped	8 celery sticks, chopped
6 juniper berries	2 tbsp plain flour
2 fresh thyme sprigs, plus	150 ml/5 fl oz double cream
extra to garnish	freshly cooked peas, to serve

cook's tip

Remove the rind from the rolled loin of pork and trim off any visible fat, if necessary, before re-rolling and tying to prepare for cooking.

1 Heat the oil with half the butter in a heavy-based saucepan or flameproof casserole. Add the pork and cook over a medium heat, turning frequently, for 5–10 minutes, or until browned. Transfer to a plate.

2 Add the shallots to the saucepan and cook, stirring frequently, for

5 minutes, or until softened. Add the juniper berries and thyme sprigs and return the pork to the saucepan, with any juices that have collected on the plate. Pour in the cider and stock, season to taste with salt and pepper, then cover and simmer for 30 minutes. Turn the pork over and add the celery. Re-cover the pan and cook for a further 40 minutes.

3 Meanwhile, make a beurre manié by mashing the remaining butter with the flour in a small bowl. Transfer the pork and celery to a platter with a slotted spoon and keep warm. Remove and discard the juniper berries and thyme. Whisk the beurre manié, a little at a time, into the simmering cooking liquid. Cook, stirring constantly, for

2 minutes, then stir in the cream and bring to the boil. Slice the pork and spoon a little of the sauce over it. Garnish with thyme sprigs and serve immediately with the celery and freshly cooked peas. Hand the remaining sauce separately.

pork chops with peppers & sweetcorn

serves 4 **prep: 10 mins**   **cook: 45 mins**

If you cook this luscious and simple dish on the hob, serve it with plenty of crusty bread. If you cook it in the oven (see Cook's Tip), serve it with baked potatoes. Either way, it makes a delicious meal.

INGREDIENTS

1 tbsp sunflower oil

4 pork chops, trimmed of visible fat

1 onion, chopped

1 garlic clove, finely chopped

1 green pepper, deseeded and sliced

1 red pepper, deseeded and sliced

325 g/11½ oz canned sweetcorn kernels

1 tbsp chopped fresh parsley

salt and pepper

mashed potato, to serve

NUTRITIONAL INFORMATION

Calories 286

Protein 24g

Carbohydrate 25g

Sugars 11g

Fat 11g

Saturates 3g

cook's tip

This casserole can also be cooked in a preheated oven, 180°C/350°F/Gas Mark 4, for 30 minutes, or until tender. Bake some potatoes alongside as an accompaniment.

1 Heat the oil in a large flameproof casserole. Add the pork chops in batches and cook over a medium heat, turning occasionally, for 5 minutes, or until browned. Transfer the chops to a plate with a slotted spoon.

2 Add the chopped onion to the casserole and cook, stirring occasionally, for

5 minutes, or until softened. Add the garlic and peppers and cook, stirring occasionally for a further 5 minutes. Stir in the sweetcorn kernels and their juices, the parsley and season to taste with salt and pepper.

3 Return the chops to the casserole, spooning the vegetable mixture over

them. Cover and simmer for 30 minutes, or until tender. Serve immediately with mashed potato.

paprika pork

cook: 35 mins   **prep: 20 mins**   **serves 4**

This is a good dish for entertaining, as it can be prepared in advance and stored in the refrigerator for up to two days. To serve, re-heat gently, then stir in the soured cream.

NUTRITIONAL INFORMATION

Calories	.478
Protein	.38g
Carbohydrates	.10g
Sugars	.4g
Fat	.30g
Saturates	.13g

INGREDIENTS

675g/1 lb 8 oz pork fillet

2 tbsp sunflower oil

25 g/1 oz butter

1 onion, chopped

1 tbsp paprika

25 g/1 oz plain flour

300 ml/10 fl oz Chicken Stock (see page 13) or 1 chicken stock cube dissolved in 300 ml/10 fl oz boiling water

4 tbsp dry sherry

115 g/4 oz mushrooms, sliced

salt and pepper

150 ml/5 fl oz soured cream

cook's tip

There are 2 kinds of paprika – sweet and hot – but both are much milder than cayenne pepper. Sweet paprika is the best choice for this recipe.

1 Cut the pork into 4-cm 1½-inch cubes. Heat the oil and butter in a large saucepan. Add the pork and cook over a medium heat, stirring, for 5 minutes, or until browned. Transfer to a plate with a slotted spoon.

2 Add the chopped onion to the saucepan and cook, stirring occasionally, for 5 minutes, or until softened. Stir in the paprika and flour and cook, stirring constantly, for 2 minutes. Gradually stir in the stock and bring to the boil, stirring constantly.

3 Return the pork to the saucepan, add the sherry and sliced mushrooms and season to taste with salt and pepper. Cover and simmer gently for 20 minutes, or until the pork is tender. Stir in the soured cream and serve.

pork & sausage bake

⏲ **cook: 1 hr 20 mins**   ⏱ **prep: 15 mins**   **serves 4**

This would be a lovely treat for a midweek family supper, and you can take time to relax while it's cooking. It is substantial enough to satisfy even the heartiest appetite.

INGREDIENTS

2 tbsp sunflower oil

25 g/1 oz butter

450 g/1 lb pork fillet or loin, cut into thin strips

1 large onion, chopped

1 red pepper, deseeded and sliced

1 orange pepper, deseeded and sliced

115 g/4 oz mushrooms, sliced

140 g/5 oz long-grain rice

425 ml/15 fl oz Beef Stock (see page 13)

225 g/8 oz smoked sausage, sliced

¼ tsp ground allspice

salt and pepper

2 tbsp chopped fresh parsley, to garnish

variation

You can use unsmoked sausages for this casserole, but you should brown them with the pork in Step 1.

cook's tip

A huge variety of smoked sausages are available, from pepperoni and many types of salami to saucisson fume aux herbes, with a herb coating.

1 Preheat the oven to 180°C/350°F/Gas Mark 4. Heat the oil and butter in a large flameproof casserole. Add the pork and cook over a medium heat, stirring, for 5 minutes, until browned. Transfer to a plate.

2 Add the onion and cook over a low heat, stirring occasionally, for 5 minutes, or until softened. Add the peppers and cook, stirring frequently, for a further 4–5 minutes. Add the mushrooms and cook for 1 minute, then stir in the rice. Cook for 1 minute, or until the grains are well coated, then add the stock and bring to the boil.

3 Return the pork to the casserole, add the sausage and allspice and season to taste with salt and pepper. Mix thoroughly, cover and cook in the preheated oven for 1 hour, or until all the liquid has been absorbed and the meat is tender. Serve immediately, garnished with chopped parsley.

spicy sausage with lentils

serves 4　　　　　**prep: 10 mins** ⏲　　　　　**cook: 25 mins** ⏲

A cross between a soup and a stew, this filling dish can be made with almost anything lurking in the storecupboard and refrigerator, so if you are short of one or two ingredients, be creative!

INGREDIENTS

1 tbsp sunflower oil

225 g/8 oz spicy sausages, sliced

115 g/4 oz rindless smoked

bacon, chopped

1 onion, chopped

6 tbsp passata

425 ml/15 fl oz Beef Stock

(see page 13)

600 g/1 lb 5 oz canned lentils,

drained and rinsed

½ tsp paprika

2 tsp red wine vinegar

salt and pepper

fresh thyme sprigs, to garnish

NUTRITIONAL INFORMATION

Calories 428

Protein 23g

Carbohydrate 23g

Sugars 5g

Fat 28g

Saturates 10g

variation

You can substitute other canned pulses for the lentils, and to turn this into a fish dish, use smoked mackerel instead of the sausages.

1 Heat the oil in a large, heavy-based saucepan. Add the sausages and bacon and cook over a medium heat, stirring, for 5 minutes, or until the bacon begins to crisp. Transfer to a plate with a slotted spoon.

2 Add the chopped onion to the saucepan and cook, stirring occasionally, for 5 minutes, or until softened. Stir in the passata and add the stock and lentils. Reduce the heat, cover and simmer for 10 minutes.

3 Return the sausage slices and bacon to the saucepan, stir in the paprika and red wine vinegar and season to taste with salt and pepper. Heat the mixture through gently for a few minutes, then serve immediately, garnished with fresh thyme sprigs.

leek & sausage tortilla

⏱ **cook: 15 mins**   ⏲ **prep: 5 mins**   **serves 2**

Serve this tasty Spanish omelette-style dish with a green salad for a nourishing and tasty supper or a delicious light lunch. It is incredibly easy and quick to put together.

NUTRITIONAL INFORMATION	
Calories	.540
Protein	.33g
Carbohydrate	.10g
Sugars	.9g
Fat	.42g
Saturates	.12g

INGREDIENTS

115 g/4 oz chorizo sausage

2 tbsp olive oil

4 leeks, thinly sliced

½ red pepper, deseeded and chopped

6 eggs

salt and pepper

variation

If you like, sprinkle the cooked tortilla with 55 g/ 2 oz of grated Cheddar cheese while still in the pan and brown under a medium grill for 2 minutes.

1 Slice the sausage. Heat the oil in a large frying pan. Add the leeks and cook over a medium heat, stirring occasionally, for 5 minutes, or until softened. Add the pepper and sausage slices and cook for 5 minutes.

2 Beat the eggs in a bowl and season to taste with salt and pepper. Pour the eggs into the frying pan and cook for a few seconds. Loosen any egg that has set at the edge of the pan with a palette knife and tilt the pan to let the uncooked egg run underneath. Continue cooking until the underside has set.

3 Remove the frying pan from the heat, place an upside-down plate on top and, holding the 2 together, invert the tortilla on to the plate. Slide it back into the frying pan and cook for a further 2 minutes, until the second side has set. Slide the tortilla out of the frying pan and cut into wedges to serve.

brunswick stew

serves 6   **prep: 15 mins** ⏲   **cook: 1 hr 20 mins** ⏲

This traditional chicken stew is a hearty dish, which is suffused with warm, spicy undertones. Serve it with salad and wholemeal rolls to make a filling, warming winter supper.

INGREDIENTS

1.8 kg/4 lb chicken pieces

salt

2 tbsp paprika

2 tbsp olive oil

25 g/1 oz butter

450 g/1 lb onions, chopped

2 yellow peppers, deseeded and chopped

400 g/14 oz canned chopped tomatoes

225 ml/8 fl oz dry white wine

450 ml/16 fl oz Chicken Stock (see page 13)

1 tbsp Worcestershire sauce

½ tsp Tabasco sauce

1 tbsp finely chopped fresh parsley

325 g/11½ oz canned sweetcorn kernels, drained

425 g/15 oz canned butter beans, drained and rinsed

2 tbsp plain flour

4 tbsp water

fresh parsley sprigs, to garnish

NUTRITIONAL INFORMATION

Calories	.670
Protein	.46g
Carbohydrate	.37g
Sugars	.14g
Fat	.36g
Saturates	.11g

variation

If you don't have time to make a chicken stock for this dish, use water instead, which works almost as well.

cook's tip

If you decide to substitute fresh tomatoes for canned tomatoes in a stew, add 1 tablespoon of tomato purée to the dish at the same time, to make sure that the flavour is strong enough.

1 Season the chicken pieces with salt and dust with paprika.

2 Heat the oil and butter in a flameproof casserole or large saucepan. Add the chicken pieces and cook over a medium heat, turning, for 10–15 minutes, or until golden. Transfer to a plate with a slotted spoon.

3 Add the onion and peppers to the casserole. Cook over a low heat, stirring occasionally, for 5 minutes, or until softened. Add the tomatoes, wine, stock, Worcestershire sauce, Tabasco sauce and parsley and bring to the boil, stirring. Return the chicken to the casserole, cover and simmer, stirring occasionally, for 30 minutes.

4 Add the sweetcorn and beans to the casserole, partially re-cover and simmer for a further 30 minutes. Place the flour and water in a small bowl and mix to make a paste. Stir a ladleful of the cooking liquid into the paste, then stir it into the stew. Cook, stirring frequently, for 5 minutes. Serve, garnished with parsley.

provençal chicken

cook: 1 hr   **prep: 20 mins**   **serves 4**

NUTRITIONAL INFORMATION

Calories 770

Protein 60g

Carbohydrate 9g

Sugars 4g

Fat 52g

Saturates 13g

variation

If you would like a little extra garlic in this dish, crush another clove into the casserole with the stock in Step 2.

This colourful dish incorporates all the wonderful flavours of southern France – olives, garlic, anchovies, tomatoes, olive oil and oregano.

INGREDIENTS

1.8 kg/4 lb chicken pieces

salt and pepper

1 garlic clove, finely chopped

3 tbsp olive oil

1 onion, finely chopped

225 g/8 oz mushrooms, halved

1 tbsp plain flour

125 ml/4 fl oz Chicken Stock

(see page 13)

175 ml/6 fl oz dry white wine

6 canned anchovy fillets, drained

3 tomatoes, peeled, deseeded and chopped

2 tsp chopped fresh oregano

6 black olives, stoned

cook's tip

Test that chicken is cooked through by piercing the thickest part with the point of a sharp knife. If the juices run clear, the chicken is ready, but if there is any trace of pink, cook for a little longer.

1 Rub the chicken pieces all over with salt, pepper and garlic. Heat the oil in a flameproof casserole. Add the chicken and cook over a medium heat, turning occasionally, for 8–10 minutes, or until golden. Add the onion, cover and cook over a low heat, stirring occasionally, for 20–25 minutes, or until cooked through and tender.

2 Transfer the chicken to a large serving plate, cover and keep warm. Add the mushrooms to the casserole and cook over a medium heat, stirring constantly, for 3 minutes. Add the flour and cook, stirring constantly, for 1 minute, then gradually stir in the stock and wine. Bring to the boil and cook, stirring, for 10 minutes, or until thickened.

3 Roughly chop 4 of the anchovies and add them to the casserole with the tomatoes, oregano and olives, then simmer for 5 minutes. Meanwhile, cut the remaining anchovies in half lengthways. Transfer the sauce and chicken to serving plates, garnish with the halved anchovies and serve immediately.

coq au vin

serves 4 **prep: 20 mins** **cook: 1 hr 15 mins**

Traditional recipes often yield wonderfully tasty results, and this dish is no exception. Serve this perennial favourite with warm French bread or garlic bread to mop up the delicious wine-flavoured juices.

INGREDIENTS

55 g/2 oz butter

2 tbsp olive oil

1.8 kg/4 lb chicken pieces

115 g/4 oz rindless smoked bacon, cut into strips

115 g/4 oz baby onions

115 g/4 oz chestnut mushrooms, halved

2 garlic cloves, finely chopped

2 tbsp brandy

225 ml/8 fl oz red wine

300 ml/10 fl oz Chicken Stock (see page 13)

1 bouquet garni

salt and pepper

2 tbsp plain flour

bay leaves, to garnish

NUTRITIONAL INFORMATION

Calories 966

Protein 62g

Carbohydrate 11g

Sugars 2g

Fat 69g

Saturates 24g

variation

You can substitute a good, full-bodied white wine, such as Chardonnay for the red wine, if you prefer.

cook's tip

If you like, cook the chicken in the oven instead of on the hob. Transfer it to a preheated oven, 160°C/325°F/Gas Mark 3, once the mixture has come to the boil in Step 2. Cook for 1 hour, then follow Step 3.

1 Melt half the butter with the olive oil in a large, flameproof casserole. Add the chicken and cook over a medium heat, stirring, for 8–10 minutes, or until golden brown all over. Add the bacon, onions, mushrooms and garlic.

2 Pour in the brandy and set it alight with a match or taper. When the flames have died down, add the wine, stock and bouquet garni and season to taste with salt and pepper. Bring to the boil, reduce the heat and simmer gently for 1 hour, or until the chicken pieces are cooked through and tender. Meanwhile, make a beurre manié by mashing the remaining butter with the flour in a small bowl.

3 Remove and discard the bouquet garni. Transfer the chicken to a large plate and keep warm. Stir the beurre manié into the casserole, a little at a time. Bring to the boil, return the chicken to the casserole and serve immediately, garnished with bay leaves.

chicken bonne femme

serves 4   **prep: 15 mins**   **cook: 1 hr 15 mins**

Bonne femme, meaning good woman, describes simple, rustic French dishes that are often served straight from the cooking dish. Chicken Bonne Femme is probably the most famous recipe.

INGREDIENTS

1.8 kg/4 lb oven-ready chicken

salt and pepper

55 g/2 oz unsalted butter

675 g/1 lb 8 oz baby onions

675 g/1 lb 8 oz new potatoes

6 rindless bacon rashers, diced

1 bouquet garni

NUTRITIONAL INFORMATION

Calories 1029

Protein 66g

Carbohydrate 41g

Sugars 12g

Fat 68g

Saturates 25g

cook's tip

If you are serving this meal at a dinner party or special lunch, give the finished dish a regal look by stuffing the neck of the cooked chicken with fresh thyme and bay sprigs.

1 Preheat the oven to 180°C/350°F/Gas Mark 4. Rinse the chicken inside and out, then pat dry with kitchen paper. Season well with salt and pepper. Melt the butter in a flameproof casserole. Add the chicken and cook over a medium heat, turning frequently, for 8–10 minutes, or until golden. Transfer to a plate.

2 Add the baby onions, potatoes and bacon to the casserole and cook over a low heat, stirring occasionally, until the onions soften and the potatoes begin to colour.

3 Return the chicken to the casserole and add the bouquet garni. Cover and cook in the preheated oven for about 1 hour, or until the

chicken is cooked through and tender. Remove and discard the bouquet garni. Transfer the chicken to a large serving platter, surround it with the vegetables and bacon and serve immediately.

chicken cacciatore

⏲ **cook: 1 hr 20 mins**   ◔ **prep: 15 mins**   **serves 4**

Cacciatore refers to the Italian term 'alla cacciatora', meaning 'hunter's-style'. This recipe follows that tradition, and is a rich and filling dish designed to give warmth and energy.

NUTRITIONAL INFORMATION

Calories	.406
Protein	.39g
Carbohydrate	.10g
Sugars	.7g
Fat	.21g
Saturates	.5g

INGREDIENTS

3 tbsp olive oil

1.8 kg/4 lb skinless chicken pieces

2 red onions, sliced

2 garlic cloves, finely chopped

400 g/14 oz canned chopped tomatoes

2 tbsp chopped fresh
flat-leaved parsley

1 tbsp sun-dried tomato purée

150 ml/5 fl oz red wine

6 fresh basil leaves

salt and pepper

fresh basil sprigs, to garnish

cook's tip

To make this casserole an even more substantial meal, serve it with freshly cooked tagliatelle or penne, or with an Italian-style olive and tomato salad.

1 Preheat the oven to 160°C/325°F/Gas Mark 3. Heat the olive oil in a flameproof casserole. Add the chicken and cook over a medium heat, stirring frequently, for 5–10 minutes, or until golden. Transfer to a plate with a slotted spoon.

2 Add the onions and garlic to the casserole and cook over a low heat, stirring occasionally, for 10 minutes, or until golden. Add the tomatoes and their juices, the parsley, tomato purée and wine, and tear in the basil leaves. Season to taste with salt and pepper.

3 Bring the mixture to the boil, then return the chicken to the casserole, pushing it down into the cooking liquid. Cover and cook in the preheated oven for 1 hour, or until the chicken is cooked through and tender. Serve immediately, garnished with fresh basil sprigs.

louisiana chicken

serves 4   **prep: 20 mins**   **cook: 1 hr 15 mins**

You can make this colourful American dish as mild or as spicy as you like by varying the quantity of chopped fresh chillies, or by adding a dash of hot Tabasco sauce before serving.

INGREDIENTS

5 tbsp sunflower oil

4 chicken portions

55 g/2 oz plain flour

1 onion, chopped

2 celery sticks, sliced

1 green pepper, deseeded and chopped

2 garlic cloves, finely chopped

2 tsp chopped fresh thyme

2 fresh red chillies, deseeded and finely chopped

400 g/14 oz canned chopped tomatoes

300 ml/10 fl oz Chicken Stock (see page 13)

salt and pepper

GARNISH

lamb's lettuce

chopped fresh thyme

NUTRITIONAL INFORMATION

Calories 573

Protein 38g

Carbohydrate 18g

Sugars 6g

Fat 40g

Saturates 9g

---

variation

Substitute prawns or crayfish for the chicken. If raw, cook until they change colour in Step 1 and return to the casserole near the end to heat through.

---

cook's tip

The success of this dish depends on the roux (the flour and fat mixture) reaching the right stage in Step 2. It should be the colour of peanut butter. Don't try to hurry the process, or the flour will burn.

1 Heat the oil in a large, heavy-based saucepan or flameproof casserole. Add the chicken and cook over a medium heat, stirring, for 5–10 minutes, or until golden. Transfer the chicken to a plate with a slotted spoon.

2 Stir the flour into the oil and cook over a very low heat, stirring constantly, for 15 minutes, or until light golden. Do not let it burn. Immediately, add the onion, celery and green pepper and cook, stirring constantly, for 2 minutes. Add the garlic, thyme and chillies and cook, stirring, for 1 minute.

3 Stir in the tomatoes and their juices, then gradually stir in the stock. Return the chicken pieces to the saucepan, cover and simmer for 45 minutes, or until the chicken is cooked through and tender. Season to taste with salt and pepper, transfer to warmed serving plates and serve immediately, garnished with some lettuce leaves and a sprinkling of chopped thyme.

chicken in white wine

 cook: 1 hr 50 mins   prep: 20 mins   serves 4

NUTRITIONAL INFORMATION

Calories 894

Protein 60g

Carbohydrates 8g

Sugars 2g

Fat 63g

Saturates 21g

Not so well known as its cousin Coq au Vin (see page 76), where chicken is cooked in red wine, this is nevertheless a popular classic and just as tasty. Serve with rice or potatoes.

INGREDIENTS

2 rindless, thick streaky bacon rashers

55 g/2 oz butter

2 tbsp olive oil

115 g/4 oz baby onions

1 garlic clove, finely chopped

1.8 kg/4 lb chicken pieces

400 ml/14 fl oz dry white wine

300 ml/10 fl oz Chicken Stock (see page 13)

1 bouquet garni

salt and pepper

115 g/4 oz button mushrooms

25 g/1 oz plain flour

fresh mixed herbs, to garnish

variation

If you prefer, replace the bouquet garni with 1 small bunch of fresh thyme and garnish the finished dish with chopped fresh flat-leaved parsley instead of the mixed herbs.

cook's tip

If there is not much room for you to stir in Step 3, transfer the chicken to serving plates and keep warm while you whisk the beurre manié into the sauce. Spoon the sauce over the chicken to serve.

1 Preheat the oven to 160°C/325°F/Gas Mark 3. Chop the bacon. Melt half the butter with the oil in a flameproof casserole. Add the bacon and cook over a medium heat, stirring, for 5–10 minutes, or until golden brown. Transfer the bacon to a large plate. Add the onions and garlic to the casserole and cook over a low heat, stirring occasionally, for 10 minutes, or until golden. Transfer to the plate. Add the chicken and cook over a medium heat, stirring constantly, for 8–10 minutes, or until golden. Transfer to the plate.

2 Drain off any excess fat from the casserole. Stir in the wine and stock and bring to the boil, scraping any sediment off the base. Add the bouquet garni and season to taste. Return the bacon, onions and chicken to the casserole. Cover and cook in the preheated oven for 1 hour. Add the mushrooms, re-cover and cook for 15 minutes. Meanwhile, make a beurre manié by mashing the remaining butter with the flour in a small bowl.

3 Remove the casserole from the oven and set over a medium heat. Remove and discard the bouquet garni. Whisk in the beurre manié, a little at a time. Bring to the boil, stirring constantly, then serve, garnished with fresh herb sprigs.

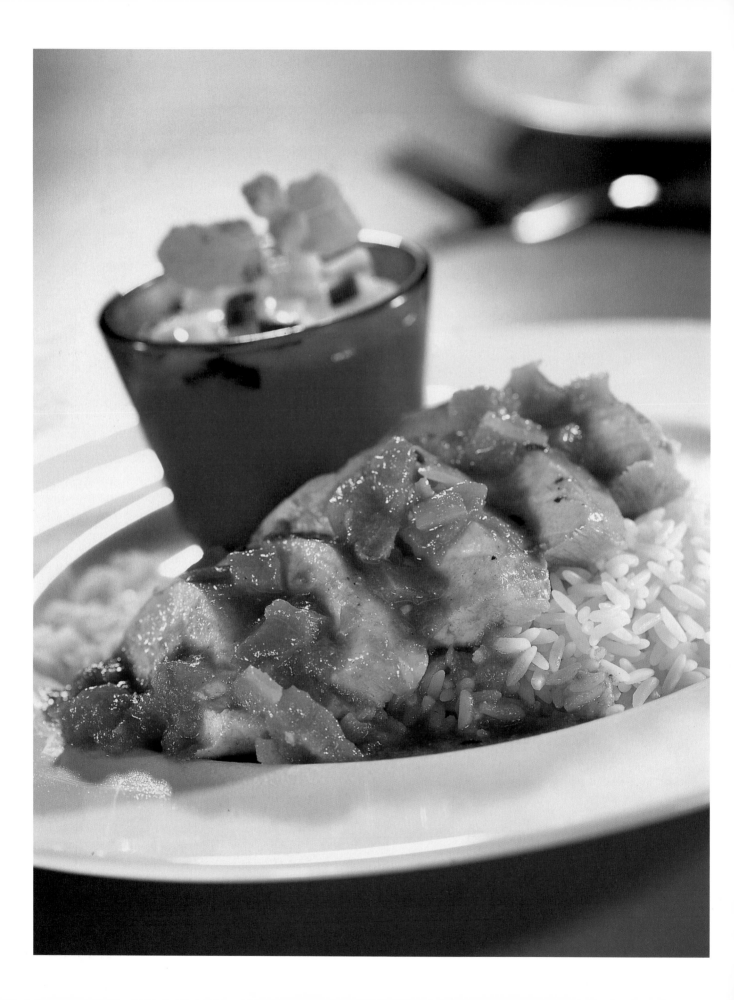

red hot chilli chicken

⏲ **cook: 40 mins**   ⏱ **prep: 20 mins**   **serves 4**

NUTRITIONAL INFORMATION

Calories 290

Protein 36g

Carbohydrate 10g

Sugars 8g

Fat 12g

Saturates 3g

variation

If you prefer a milder version of this dish, try to find Ancho or Anaheim varieties of chillies and deseed them before using.

This is a really fiery curry with a wonderfully aromatic, home-made chilli paste, for those who like it hot. You can mix the spice paste by hand with a pestle and mortar if you have to, but it is much quicker and easier to use a blender or food processor.

INGREDIENTS

1 tbsp curry paste

2 fresh green chillies, chopped

5 dried red chillies

2 tbsp tomato purée

2 garlic cloves, chopped

1 tsp chilli powder

pinch of sugar

salt

2 tbsp groundnut or sunflower oil

½ tsp cumin seeds

1 onion, chopped

2 curry leaves

1 tsp ground cumin

1 tsp ground coriander

½ tsp ground turmeric

400 g/14 oz canned chopped tomatoes

150 ml/5 fl oz Chicken Stock

(see page 13)

4 skinless, boneless chicken breasts

1 tsp garam masala

TO SERVE

freshly cooked rice

natural yogurt

cook's tip

Indian cooks usually make their own garam masala, but it is available ready-made from supermarkets and specialist Indian food stores.

1 To make the chilli paste, place the curry paste, fresh and dried chillies, tomato purée, garlic, chilli powder and sugar in a blender or food processor and add a pinch of salt. Process to a smooth paste.

2 Heat the oil in a large, heavy-based saucepan. Add the cumin seeds and cook over a medium heat, stirring constantly, for 2 minutes, or until they begin to pop and release their aroma. Add the onion and curry leaves and cook, stirring, for 5 minutes.

3 Add the chilli paste and cook for 2 minutes, then stir in the ground cumin, coriander and turmeric and cook for a further 2 minutes.

4 Add the tomatoes and their juices and the stock. Bring to the boil, then reduce the heat and simmer for 5 minutes. Add the chicken and garam masala, cover and simmer gently for 20 minutes, or until the chicken is cooked through and tender. Serve immediately with freshly cooked rice and yogurt.

✗ chicken pasanda

serves 4

prep: 20 mins, plus 2–3 hrs marinating

cook: 25 mins

This Balti dish is traditionally cooked and served in a karahi – a pan similar in shape to a wok. If you have neither a karahi nor a wok, use a large, heavy-based frying pan instead.

INGREDIENTS

4 cardamom pods

6 black peppercorns

½ cinnamon stick

½ tsp cumin seeds

2 tsp garam masala

1 tsp chilli powder

1 tsp grated fresh root ginger

1 garlic clove, very finely chopped

4 tbsp thick natural yogurt

salt

675 g/1 lb 8 oz skinless, boneless chicken, diced

5 tbsp groundnut oil

2 onions, finely chopped

3 fresh green chillies, deseeded and chopped

2 tbsp chopped fresh coriander

125 ml/4 fl oz single cream

fresh coriander sprigs, to garnish

NUTRITIONAL INFORMATION

Calories 426

Protein 41g

Carbohydrate 8g

Sugars 7g

Fat 26g

Saturates 7g

---

variation

If you cannot find any groundnut oil at your local food store, you can substitute sunflower oil instead.

---

cook's tip

When this is served in the traditional way, all the diners tear off pieces of naan bread and scoop out some of the mixture from the karahi.

1 Place the cardamom pods in a non-metallic dish with the peppercorns, cinnamon, cumin, garam masala, chilli powder, ginger, garlic, yogurt and a pinch of salt. Add the chicken pieces and stir well to coat. Cover and leave to marinate in the refrigerator for 2–3 hours.

2 Heat the oil in a preheated wok or karahi. Add the onions and cook over a low heat, stirring occasionally, for 5 minutes, or until softened, then add the chicken pieces and marinade and cook over a medium heat, stirring, for 15 minutes, or until the chicken is cooked through.

3 Stir in the fresh chillies and coriander and pour in the cream. Heat through gently, but do not let it boil. Garnish with fresh coriander and serve immediately.

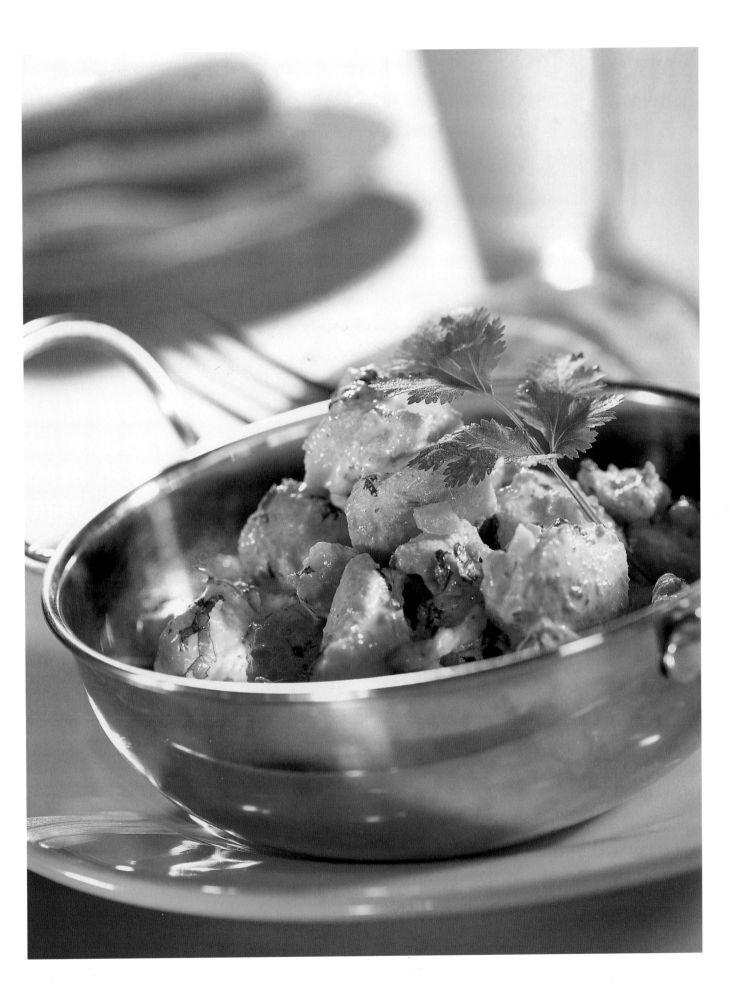

italian turkey steaks

serves 4   **prep: 10 mins**   **cook: 50 mins**

This lively summer dish is simplicity itself, but tastes really wonderful and makes a surprisingly substantial main course.

INGREDIENTS

1 tbsp olive oil

4 turkey escalopes or steaks

2 red peppers

1 red onion

2 garlic cloves, finely chopped

300 ml/10 fl oz passata

150 ml/5 fl oz medium white wine

1 tbsp chopped fresh marjoram

salt and pepper

400 g/14 oz canned cannellini beans, drained and rinsed

3 tbsp fresh white breadcrumbs

fresh basil sprigs, to garnish

NUTRITIONAL INFORMATION

Calories	.264
Protein	.33g
Carbohydrate	.18g
Sugars	.11g
Fat	.5g
Saturates	.1g

variation

Soak 15 g/½ oz of dried porcini mushrooms in boiling water to cover for 20 minutes. Drain and slice, then add with the onion and peppers in Step 2.

1 Heat the oil in a flameproof casserole or heavy-based frying pan. Add the turkey escalopes and cook over a medium heat for 5–10 minutes, turning occasionally, until golden. Transfer to a plate.

2 Deseed and slice the red peppers. Slice the onion, add to the frying pan

with the red peppers and cook over a low heat, stirring occasionally, for 5 minutes, or until softened. Add the garlic and cook for a further 2 minutes.

3 Return the turkey to the frying pan and add the passata, wine and marjoram. Season to taste with salt and pepper. Bring to the boil, then

reduce the heat, cover and simmer, stirring occasionally, for 25–30 minutes, or until the turkey is cooked through and tender.

4 Stir in the cannellini beans and simmer for a further 5 minutes. Sprinkle the breadcrumbs over the top and place under a preheated grill for 2–3 minutes, or until

golden. Serve, garnished with fresh basil sprigs.

turkey in a piquant sauce

🍳 **cook: 1 hr 45 mins**   ⏱ **prep: 20 mins**   **serves 4**

Turkey portions make an easy and economical family supper. Here they are served in a delicious tomato and pepper sauce.

NUTRITIONAL INFORMATION	
Calories	290
Protein	29g
Carbohydrate	13g
Sugars	6g
Fat	14g
Saturates	5g

INGREDIENTS

2 tbsp plain flour

salt and pepper

1 kg/2 lb 4 oz turkey pieces

25 g/1 oz butter

1 tbsp sunflower oil

2 onions, sliced

1 garlic clove, finely chopped

1 red pepper, deseeded and sliced

400 g/14 oz canned chopped tomatoes

1 bouquet garni

150 ml/5 fl oz Chicken Stock

(see page 13)

2 tbsp chopped fresh parsley,

to garnish

variation

This recipe also works just as well with chicken pieces. Chicken is more tender than turkey, so reduce the simmering time at the end of Step 3 to 45 minutes.

1 Spread the flour on a plate and season with salt and pepper. Coat the turkey pieces in the seasoned flour, shaking off any excess.

2 Melt the butter with the oil in a flameproof casserole or large saucepan. Add the turkey and cook over a medium heat, stirring, for 5–10 minutes, or until golden.

Transfer the turkey pieces to a plate with a slotted spoon and keep warm. Add the onions, garlic and red pepper to the casserole and cook, stirring occasionally, for 5 minutes, or until softened. Sprinkle in any remaining flour and cook, stirring constantly, for 1 minute.

3 Return the turkey pieces to the casserole, then add the tomatoes and their juices, the bouquet garni and stock. Bring to the boil, stirring constantly, then cover and simmer for 1¼ hours, or until the turkey is cooked through and tender.

4 Transfer the turkey to a serving platter with a slotted spoon. Remove and discard the bouquet garni.

Return the sauce to the boil and cook until reduced and thickened. Season to taste with salt and pepper and pour over the turkey. Serve immediately, garnished with parsley.

mexican turkey

cook: 1 hr 10 mins   **prep: 15 mins**   **serves 4**

NUTRITIONAL INFORMATION

Calories 355

Protein 38g

Carbohydrate 25g

Sugars 14g

Fat 13g

Saturates 3g

variation

You can also prepare this dish with 675 g/1 lb 8 oz of diced, lean beef, but you will need to allow an extra 15 minutes cooking time.

Using chocolate in savoury dishes is a Mexican tradition and, while it may sound strange, it gives the meat a very rich flavour. Mexican chocolate often has cinnamon incorporated into it, but you can use ordinary plain chocolate and ground cinnamon for this dish.

INGREDIENTS

55 g/2 oz plain flour

salt and pepper

4 turkey breast fillets

3 tbsp corn oil

1 onion, thinly sliced

1 red pepper, deseeded and sliced

300 ml/10 fl oz Chicken Stock

(see page 13)

25 g/1 oz raisins

4 tomatoes, peeled, deseeded and chopped

1 tsp chilli powder

½ tsp ground cinnamon

pinch of ground cumin

25 g/1 oz plain chocolate, finely chopped or grated

chopped fresh coriander, to garnish

cook's tip

For the best flavour, choose the best quality plain chocolate you can find for this dish. It should contain a minimum of 70 per cent cocoa solids.

1 Preheat the oven to 160°C/325°F/Gas Mark 3. Spread the flour on a plate and season with salt and pepper. Coat the turkey fillets in the seasoned flour, shaking off any excess.

2 Heat the oil in a flameproof casserole. Add the turkey fillets and cook over a medium heat, turning occasionally, for 5–10 minutes, or until golden. Transfer onto a plate with a slotted spoon.

3 Add the onion and red pepper to the casserole. Cook over a low heat, stirring occasionally, for 5 minutes, or until softened. Sprinkle in any remaining seasoned flour and cook, stirring constantly, for 1 minute. Gradually stir in the stock, then add the raisins, chopped tomatoes, chilli powder, cinnamon, cumin and chocolate. Season to taste with salt and pepper. Bring to the boil, stirring constantly.

4 Return the turkey to the casserole, cover and cook in the preheated oven for 50 minutes. Serve immediately, garnished with coriander.

fish & seafood

The range of seafood available these days is immense, but sometimes it is difficult to know how to cook unfamiliar fish. The answer might be to put it into a pot and make a fabulous stew – Fishermen's Stew (see page 96) is incredibly easy to make and equally delicious.

This section is packed with recipes with an international flavour, from Boston Fish Pie (see page 102), Thai Prawn Curry (see page 108) and the Swedish casserole Jansson's Temptation (see page 106) to Mediterranean delights, such as Swordfish with Tomatoes & Olives (see page 98). A little sophistication is also introduced with the traditional French dish, Moules Marinières (see page 107).

The following pages include ideas for preparing every kind of seafood, from prawns and tuna to monkfish and squid – and not an unhealthy chip in sight. Whether you are looking for a hot curry, a warming casserole or a traditional paella, you are bound to find a meal to suit every occasion.

cod in lemon & parsley

⏱ **cook: 25 mins**　　　⏲ **prep: 15 mins**　　　**serves 4**

NUTRITIONAL INFORMATION	
Calories	.248
Protein	.34g
Carbohydrate	.9g
Sugars	.7g
Fat	.7g
Saturates	.1g

variation

If you want to substitute another white fish for the cod, try firm steaks of whiting, halibut or haddock.

This is a very simple way to cook fish, with lovely, refreshing Mediterranean flavours. Any firm white fish steaks or fillets are equally good at absorbing the flavours of this delicious dish.

INGREDIENTS

2 onions

1 garlic clove

2 tbsp olive oil

4 tomatoes, peeled and quartered

grated rind and juice of ½ lemon

6 tbsp dry white wine

3 tbsp chopped fresh mixed herbs, such as parsley, thyme and chives

4 cod steaks, about 175 g/6 oz each

salt and pepper

fresh thyme sprigs, to garnish

cook's tip

This is an excellent emergency dish to have on standby when you have unexpected visitors, and it tastes just as good made with frozen fish. Thaw under cold – not hot – water, or in the microwave before cooking.

1 Finely chop the onions and garlic. Heat the olive oil in a large, heavy-based frying pan. Add the onion and cook over a low heat, stirring occasionally, for 5 minutes, or until softened.

2 Add the garlic and tomatoes and cook for 3–4 minutes. Add the lemon rind and juice, white wine, chopped herbs and cod steaks, and season to taste with salt and pepper.

3 Set the heat as low as possible, then cover the frying pan and simmer gently for 15 minutes, or until the fish is cooked through and flakes easily when tested with the point of a knife. Serve immediately, garnished with fresh thyme sprigs.

fishermen's stew

serves 6   **prep: 20 mins** ⟲   **cook: 35 mins** ⟳

This richly flavoured mixture of fish and shellfish is a fabulous way to feed guests, as it is easy to prepare and needs no more accompaniment than chunks of fresh bread or crusty rolls.

INGREDIENTS

1.5 kg/3 lb 5 oz live mussels

3 tbsp olive oil

2 onions, chopped

3 garlic cloves, finely chopped

1 red pepper, deseeded and sliced

3 carrots, chopped

800 g/1 lb 12 oz canned

chopped tomatoes

125 ml/4 fl oz dry white wine

2 tbsp tomato purée

1 tbsp chopped fresh dill

2 tbsp chopped fresh parsley

1 tbsp chopped fresh thyme

1 tbsp fresh basil leaves, plus

extra to garnish

900 g/2 lb white fish fillets,

cut into chunks

450 g/1 lb raw prawns

350 ml/12 fl oz Fish Stock

(see page 13) or water

salt and pepper

variation

If you can't find raw prawns, use cooked ones and add them for the last 2–3 minutes of the cooking time in Step 4. They need only heat through.

cook's tip

When you buy live mussels, make sure that the shells are pristine, not cracked or broken. Always prepare them carefully, following the instructions in Steps 1 and 4.

1 Clean the mussels by scrubbing or scraping the shells and pulling off any beards. Discard any with broken shells or any that refuse to close when tapped with a knife. Rinse the mussels under cold running water.

2 Heat the oil in a flameproof casserole. Add the onions, garlic, red pepper and carrots and cook over a low heat, stirring occasionally, for 5 minutes, or until softened.

3 Add the tomatoes and their juices, the white wine, tomato purée, dill, parsley and thyme, and tear in the basil leaves. Bring to the boil, then reduce the heat and simmer for 20 minutes.

4 Add the chunks of fish, mussels, prawns and stock and season to taste with salt and pepper. Return the stew to the boil and simmer for 6–8 minutes, or until the prawns have turned pink and the mussel shells have opened. Discard any shells that remain closed. Serve immediately, garnished with basil leaves.

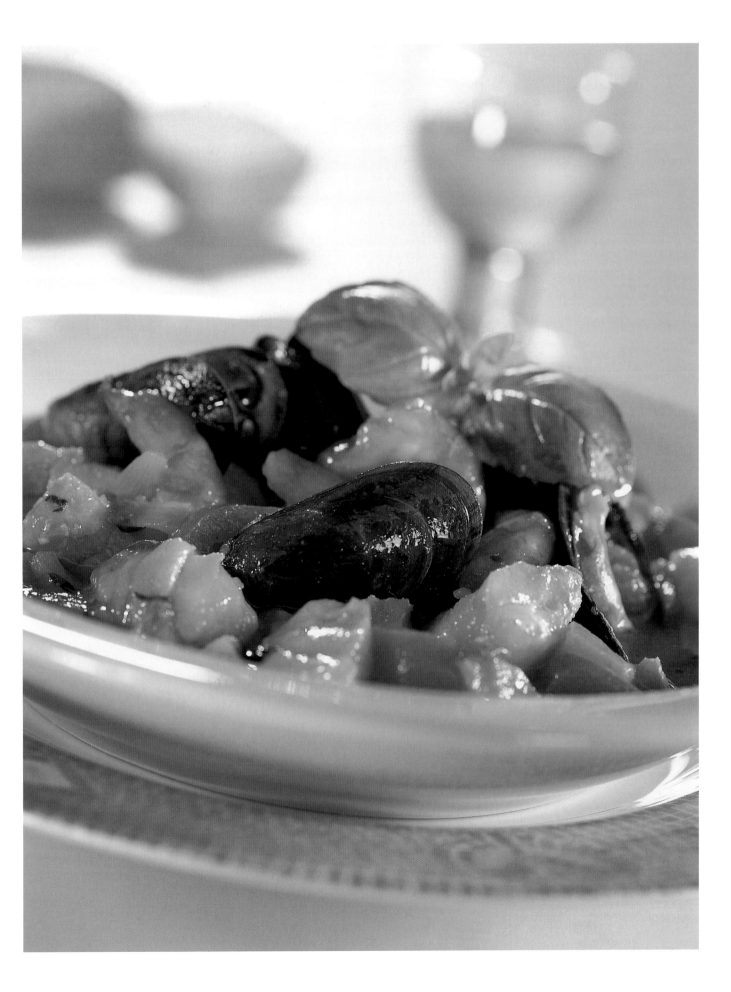

swordfish with tomatoes & olives

serves 4   **prep: 15 mins**   **cook: 40 mins**

Treat your family to this wonderful dish for an alfresco supper. Its flavour is very distinctive, so serve it with a side dish that won't compete – such as a straightforward green salad.

INGREDIENTS

2 tbsp olive oil

1 onion, finely chopped

1 celery stick, finely chopped

115 g/4 oz green olives, stoned

450 g/1 lb tomatoes, chopped

3 tbsp bottled capers, drained

salt and pepper

4 swordfish steaks,
about 140 g/5 oz each

fresh flat-leaved parsley sprigs,
to garnish

NUTRITIONAL INFORMATION

Calories 250

Protein 26g

Carbohydrate 5g

Sugars 4g

Fat 14g

Saturates 3g

variation

Swordfish is a very firm, meaty fish, but you could substitute cod steaks, monkfish tail or even shark steaks, if you like.

1 Heat the oil in a large, heavy-based frying pan. Add the onion and celery and cook over a low heat, stirring occasionally, for 5 minutes, or until softened. Meanwhile, roughly chop half the olives. Stir the chopped and whole olives into the saucepan with the tomatoes and capers and

season to taste with salt and pepper. Bring to the boil, then reduce the heat, cover and simmer gently, stirring occasionally, for 15 minutes.

2 Add the swordfish steaks to the pan and return to the boil. Cover and simmer, turning the fish once,

for 20 minutes, or until the fish is cooked and the flesh flakes easily. Transfer the fish to serving plates and spoon the sauce over them. Garnish with fresh parsley sprigs and serve immediately.

griddled tuna with baby vegetables

cook: 6–8 mins   **prep: 5 mins, plus 1 hr marinating**   **serves 4**

Tuna is often served in the same way as steak – that is, slightly rare in the middle. If you prefer your fish well done, then cook the tuna for a further 1–2 minutes on each side.

NUTRITIONAL INFORMATION	
Calories	.400
Protein	.45g
Carbohydrate	.6g
Sugars	.3g
Fat	.23g
Saturates	.4g

INGREDIENTS

5 tbsp olive oil

2 tbsp lemon juice

1 tbsp lime juice

salt and pepper

4 tuna steaks, about 175 g/6 oz each

8 baby leeks

8 asparagus spears

8 cherry tomatoes

4 baby courgettes, halved lengthways

cook's tip

Depending on the size of your griddle pan, you may need to cook this dish in 2 batches. If you do not have a griddle pan, you can use a large, heavy-based frying pan.

1 Place 4 tablespoons of the oil in a shallow, non-metallic dish with the lemon juice and lime juice, and season to taste. Add the fish, turning to coat, then cover and leave to marinate in the refrigerator for 1 hour.

2 Heat a griddle pan and brush with the remaining oil. Drain the tuna steaks, season to taste with salt and pepper and add to the pan. Cook over a high heat for 3–4 minutes, then turn.

3 Add the baby leeks, asparagus, cherry tomatoes and baby courgettes. Cook for a further 3–4 minutes, then serve.

paella del mar

serves 6   **prep: 45 mins** ⏱   **cook: 25–30 mins** ⏱

Paella is actually the name of the pan in which this famous Spanish dish is cooked – a large, heavy-based frying pan or casserole is a good substitute. This fish and shellfish version comes from Valencia.

INGREDIENTS

450 g/1 lb live mussels	175 g/6 oz monkfish fillet,
6 squid	cut into chunks
125 ml/4 fl oz olive oil	175 g/6 oz red mullet fillet,
1 Spanish onion, chopped	cut into chunks
2 garlic cloves, finely chopped	175 g/6 oz cod fillet, cut into chunks
1 red pepper, deseeded and	500 ml/18 fl oz Fish Stock (see page 13)
cut into strips	115 g/4 oz fresh or frozen green
1 green pepper, deseeded	beans, halved
and cut into strips	115 g/4 oz fresh or frozen peas
400 g/14 oz risotto rice	6 canned artichoke hearts, drained
2 tomatoes, peeled and chopped	¼ tsp saffron threads
1 tbsp tomato purée	salt and pepper
	12 raw Mediterranean or tiger prawns

NUTRITIONAL INFORMATION

Calories 623

Protein 48g

Carbohydrate 68g

Sugars 7g

Fat 19g

Saturates 2g

variation

Any kind of firm-fleshed fish can be used in this paella. You could also experiment with other vegetables, such as chopped courgettes or asparagus.

cook's tip

Authentic paella is made with round grain Valencia rice, but this is difficult to obtain outside Spain. Risotto rice is a good substitute, or you could use long-grain rice, although this will tend to stick to the pan.

1 Clean the mussels by scrubbing or scraping the shells and pulling off any beards. Discard any with broken shells or any that refuse to close when tapped with a knife. Rinse the mussels under cold running water.

2 To prepare each squid, pull the pouch and tentacles apart, then remove the innards from the pouch. Slice the tentacles away from the head and discard the head. Rinse the pouch and tentacles under cold running water.

3 Heat the oil in a paella pan or flameproof casserole. Add the onion, garlic and peppers and cook over a medium heat, stirring, for 5 minutes, or until softened.

Add the squid and cook for 2 minutes. Add the rice and cook, stirring, until transparent and coated with oil.

4 Add the tomatoes, tomato purée and fish and cook for 3 minutes, then add the stock. Gently stir in the beans, peas, artichoke hearts and saffron and season to taste with salt and pepper.

5 Arrange the mussels around the edge of the pan and top the mixture with the prawns. Bring to the boil, reduce the heat and simmer, shaking the pan from time to time, for 15–20 minutes, or until the rice is tender. Discard any mussels that remain closed. Serve straight from the pan.

boston fish pie

⏱ **cook: 40 mins**   ◔ **prep: 15 mins**   **serves 6**

The Massachusetts city of Boston has been described as 'the home of the bean and the cod'. This may not be glamorous, but this unusual fish pie does demonstrate that it is a tasty and filling combination.

NUTRITIONAL INFORMATION

Calories 413

Protein 41g

Carbohydrate 33g

Sugars 9g

Fat 14g

Saturates 6g

variation

You could use an equal mixture of fresh and smoked cod and add a few juniper berries with the parsley, if you would like a stronger flavour.

INGREDIENTS

25 g/1 oz butter, plus extra for greasing

2 onions, chopped

1 kg/2 lb 4 oz cod fillet, skinned and cut into strips

4 rindless streaky bacon rashers, cut into strips

2 tbsp chopped fresh parsley

salt and pepper

400 g/14 oz canned haricot beans, drained and rinsed

600 ml/1 pint milk

500 g/1 lb 2 oz potatoes, very thinly sliced

fresh parsley sprigs, to garnish

cook's tip

If you like, before baking in the oven, cover the casserole with foil, then remove the foil for the last 10 minutes of cooking time to crisp up the potatoes.

1 Preheat the oven to 180°C/350°F/Gas Mark 4. Lightly grease a flameproof casserole with a little butter. Arrange the onions in the base and cover with the strips of fish and bacon. Sprinkle with the parsley and season to taste with salt and pepper.

2 Add the haricot beans, then pour in the milk. Arrange the potato slices, overlapping them slightly, to cover the entire surface of the pie.

3 Dot the potato slices with the butter. Bake the pie in the preheated oven for 40 minutes, or until the potatoes are crisp and golden. Garnish with parsley sprigs and serve immediately.

monkfish with onions & coriander

cook: 20 mins

prep: 15 mins, plus 1 hr marinating

serves 4

Monkfish is popular not just because of its fine flavour and firm texture, but also because there are none of the little bones that sometimes put people off fish. It is a meaty fish, so all you need to accompany it is a simple green salad.

INGREDIENTS

1 kg/2 lb 4 oz monkfish tail

4 tbsp lime juice

1 garlic clove, finely chopped

1 tsp ground cumin

1 tsp paprika

salt and pepper

1 Spanish onion, sliced into rings

2 fresh red chillies, deseeded and finely chopped

1 tbsp chopped fresh coriander

2 tbsp olive oil

fresh coriander leaves, to garnish

variation

Substitute green chillies for the red chillies if you would prefer a slightly more bitter spiciness in this dish.

cook's tip

Be careful not to leave the monkfish fillets to marinate for more than 1 hour, otherwise the lime juice will begin to 'cook' the flesh.

1 Preheat the oven to 220°C/425°F/Gas Mark 7. Remove the grey membrane that covers the monkfish tail with a sharp knife, then cut along one side of the central bone to remove the fillet of flesh. Repeat on the other side to remove the other fillet from the bone, then tie the 2 fillets together with kitchen string. Transfer the tied fillets to a shallow, non-metallic, ovenproof dish.

2 Place the lime juice, garlic, cumin and paprika in a bowl, stir to mix, and season to taste with salt and pepper. Spoon the marinade over the monkfish, cover and leave to marinate in the refrigerator for 1 hour.

3 Sprinkle the onion rings, chillies and the chopped coriander over the fish and drizzle with the oil. Roast in the preheated oven for 20 minutes, or until cooked through and the flesh flakes easily. Cut the fish into slices, garnish with fresh coriander leaves and serve.

jansson's temptation

serves 4   **prep: 10 mins**   **cook: 1 hr**

Jansson was a Swedish opera singer, as famous for his liaisons as his singing. Favoured guests visited his rooms after a performance, where he cooked for them. This was one of the meals they enjoyed.

INGREDIENTS

40 g/1½ oz butter, plus extra
for greasing
14 anchovy fillets
450 g/1 lb potatoes, grated
2 onions, sliced
1 garlic clove, finely chopped
1 tbsp chopped fresh parsley
pepper
300 ml/10 fl oz single cream
fresh parsley sprigs, to garnish

NUTRITIONAL INFORMATION

Calories	.373
Protein	.8g
Carbohydrate	.29g
Sugars	.8g
Fat	.26g
Saturates	.15g

cook's tip

If you use canned anchovy fillets, you can drizzle a little of the oil over the potatoes before adding the cream in Step 2. If using salted anchovy fillets, soak them in water or milk before filleting them.

1 Preheat the oven to 200°C/400°F/Gas Mark 6. Generously grease an ovenproof dish with butter. Cut each anchovy fillet into 4 pieces.

2 Layer the grated potatoes, onion slices, garlic, parsley and anchovies in the dish, ending with a layer of potatoes, seasoning each layer with pepper. Pour half the cream over the top and dot with the butter.

3 Bake in the preheated oven for 35–40 minutes, or until the potatoes are just coloured, then pour over the remaining cream and bake for a further 20–25 minutes, or until the topping is golden and tender. Serve immediately, garnished with fresh parsley sprigs.

moules marinières

⏱ **cook: 10 mins**   ⏲ **prep: 25 mins**   **serves 4**

Served with plenty of fresh crusty French bread, this is a shellfish-lover's feast. The only extra treat you need to make this into a perfect meal is a glass of chilled white wine.

NUTRITIONAL INFORMATION

Calories 185

Protein 26g

Carbohydrate 2g

Sugars 1g

Fat 3g

Saturates 1g

INGREDIENTS

2 kg/4 lb 8 oz live mussels

300 ml/10 fl oz dry white wine

6 shallots, finely chopped

1 bouquet garni

pepper

crusty bread, to serve

cook's tip

Never eat mussels that you have collected from the beach yourself, as they may have been polluted and could cause serious illness.

1 Clean the mussels by scrubbing or scraping the shells and pulling off any beards. Discard any with broken shells or any that refuse to close when tapped with a knife. Rinse the mussels under cold running water.

2 Pour the wine into a large, heavy-based saucepan, add the shallots and bouquet garni and season to taste with pepper. Bring to the boil over a medium heat. Add the mussels, cover tightly and cook, shaking the saucepan occasionally, for 5 minutes. Remove and discard the bouquet garni and any mussels that remain closed.

3 Divide the mussels between 4 soup plates with a slotted spoon. Tilt the casserole to let any sand settle, then spoon the cooking liquid over the mussels and serve immediately with bread.

thai prawn curry

cook: 10 mins   **prep: 15 mins**   **serves 4**

variation

Replace the fresh basil leaves with the same amount of fresh coriander leaves. If you prefer a milder curry, deseed the fresh chilli before slicing.

Thai cooking is renowned for its subtle blending of aromatic spices, and this mouthwatering curry is no exception.

INGREDIENTS

450 g/1 lb raw tiger prawns

2 tbsp groundnut oil

2 tbsp Thai green curry paste

4 kaffir lime leaves, shredded

1 lemon grass stalk, chopped

225 ml/8 fl oz coconut milk

2 tbsp Thai fish sauce

½ cucumber, deseeded and cut into batons

12 fresh basil leaves, plus extra to garnish

2 fresh green chillies, sliced

cook's tip

Three types of basil are used in Thailand: hairy (*bai mangluk*), sweet (*bai horapa*) and Thai or holy basil (*bai grapao*). They are all more strongly flavoured than western basil.

1 Peel and devein the prawns. Heat the groundnut oil in a preheated wok or heavy-based frying pan. Add the curry paste and cook over a medium heat for 1 minute, or until it is bubbling and releases its aroma.

2 Add the prawns, lime leaves and lemon grass and stir-fry for 2 minutes, or until the prawns have turned pink.

3 Stir in the coconut milk and bring to the boil,

then reduce the heat and simmer, stirring occasionally, for 5 minutes. Stir in the fish sauce, cucumber and basil. Transfer to a warmed serving dish. Scatter over the chilli slices, garnish with fresh basil leaves and serve.

sweet & sour prawns

serves 4   **prep: 10 mins** ⏲   **cook: 5 mins** ⏲

The flavours of dark soy sauce and sesame oil are set off by tangy fresh root ginger and rich muscovado sugar in this Eastern stir-fry.

INGREDIENTS

4 spring onions, finely chopped, plus extra to garnish

2 tsp finely chopped fresh root ginger

450 g/1 lb cooked tiger prawns

1 tbsp groundnut or sunflower oil

2 tbsp dark soy sauce

2 tbsp muscovado sugar

3 tbsp rice vinegar

1 tbsp Chinese rice wine

125 ml/4 fl oz Fish or Chicken Stock (see page 13)

1 tsp cornflour

1–2 tbsp water

dash of sesame oil

shredded Chinese leaves, to serve

variation

To serve with noodles, break up 225 g/ 8 oz of rice vermicelli into short lengths, heat 4 tablespoons of oil in the wok and stir-fry in batches.

cook's tip

Rather than discarding prawn heads and shells, you can use them to make a delicately flavoured shellfish stock by simmering them gently in enough water to cover.

1 Finely chop the spring onions, and peel and finely chop the fresh root ginger. Peel and devein the prawns, pat dry with kitchen paper and reserve.

2 Heat the oil in a preheated wok or large frying pan. Add the spring onions and ginger and stir-fry over a high heat for 1 minute.

Add the soy sauce, sugar, vinegar, rice wine and stock and bring to the boil.

3 Place the cornflour and water in a small bowl and combine to make a paste. Stir 1 tablespoon of the paste into the sauce and add the prawns. Cook, stirring, until slightly thickened and smooth. Sprinkle with sesame oil.

4 Make a bed of Chinese leaves on 4 serving plates and top with prawns and sauce. Garnish with shredded spring onion tassels and serve immediately.

griddled squid

⏲ **cook: 5–10 mins**   ⏱ **prep: 15 mins**   **serves 4**

variation

Chop 100g/3½ oz of thawed peeled prawns with 1 tablespoon of chopped dill and 2 chopped shallots. Use to fill the pouches. Continue from Step 2.

This recipe works best with delicate baby squid, but if you can obtain only larger squid, slice the bodies into thick rings and cut the tentacles in half before you begin cooking.

INGREDIENTS

450 g/1 lb baby squid

2 tbsp olive oil

1 bunch of fresh parsley, finely chopped

4 garlic cloves, crushed

1 tbsp grated lemon rind

1 tbsp lemon juice

salt and pepper

fresh flat-leaved parsley sprigs, to garnish

cook's tip

If you don't want to use a griddle pan for this dish, you can also cook the squid under a preheated hot grill or on a lit barbecue, turning frequently and brushing with olive oil.

1 To prepare each squid, pull the pouch and tentacles apart, then remove the remaining innards from the pouch. Slice the tentacles away from the head and discard the head. Rinse the pouch and tentacles under cold running water.

2 Heat a griddle pan and brush with oil. Add the squid pouches and tentacles and cook over a medium heat, turning and brushing with more oil occasionally, for 5–10 minutes, or until golden brown. Divide between 4 serving plates.

3 Place the parsley, garlic and lemon rind in a small bowl and stir to mix. Sprinkle the lemon juice over the squid and season to taste with salt and pepper. Sprinkle the parsley mixture over the squid, garnish with parsley sprigs and serve warm.

vegetarian

Nutritionists tell us that we should eat more vegetables, but it isn't always easy to persuade the family to eat up their greens, especially if they are sitting in an unappetising heap on the side of the plate. This chapter provides the answer, with a spectacular collection of mouthwatering vegetable dishes, from Mediterranean-style Greek Beans (see page 116) to a delicious and unusual Winter Vegetable Cobbler (see page 127).

Beans, lentils, peppers, courgettes, aubergines, broccoli, cauliflower, onions, tomatoes and even the humble potato take a starring role, and are combined with each other for a colourful, melt-in-the-mouth medley which will satisfy even the hungriest appetite. If you are in the mood for something hot, try Vegetable Chilli (see page 120), Yellow Curry (see page 124) or Spiced Cashew Nut Curry (see page 125). If you are looking for something a little more comforting, Cauliflower Bake (see page 128) or Pepper & Mushroom Hash (see page 117) will fit the bill perfectly.

A vegetarian main course is an easy way to ring the changes in the weekly menu, and nut- or pulse-based dishes can be just as nutritious as a meat or fish dish. Whatever your favourite vegetable, there will be something in this section to tempt even the keenest meat-eater to try something a little different.

greek beans

serves 4   **prep: 5 mins**   **cook: 1 min**

This dish contains many typical Greek flavours, such as lemon and garlic, for a really flavoursome recipe. The fresh oregano and black olives give it a real taste of the Mediterranean.

INGREDIENTS

400 g/14 oz canned haricot
beans, drained
1 tbsp olive oil
3 garlic cloves, crushed
425 ml/15 fl oz Vegetable Stock
(see page 13)
1 bay leaf
2 fresh oregano sprigs
1 tbsp tomato purée
juice of 1 lemon
1 small red onion, chopped
25 g/1 oz stoned black olives, halved
salt and pepper

NUTRITIONAL INFORMATION

Calories 115

Protein 6g

Carbohydrate 15g

Sugars 4g

Fat 4g

Saturates 0.6g

cook's tip

You can substitute other canned beans for the haricot beans – try cannellini or black-eyed beans or chickpeas. Drain and rinse them before use, because canned beans often have sugar or salt added.

1 Put the haricot beans into a flameproof casserole dish, add the oil and crushed garlic and cook over a low heat, stirring occasionally, for 4–5 minutes.

2 Add the stock, bay leaf, oregano, tomato purée, lemon juice and red onion and stir to mix. Cover and simmer for 1 hour, or until the sauce has thickened.

3 Stir in the black olives, then season the beans to taste with salt and pepper. The dish is delicious served either warm or cold.

pepper & mushroom hash

⏱ **cook: 30 mins**   ⏱ **prep: 5 mins**   **serves 4**

This quick and easy-to-prepare one-pan dish is ideal for an evening snack. Packed with colour and flavour, it is an extremely versatile recipe – you can add whichever vegetables you have to hand.

NUTRITIONAL INFORMATION

Calories 182

Protein 5g

Carbohydrate 34g

Sugars 6g

Fat 4g

Saturates 0.5g

INGREDIENTS

675 g/1 lb 8 oz potatoes, cut into cubes

salt and pepper

1 tbsp olive oil

2 garlic cloves, crushed

1 green pepper, deseeded
and cut into cubes

1 yellow pepper, deseeded
and cut into cubes

3 tomatoes, diced

75 g/2¾ oz button mushrooms, halved

1 tbsp Worcestershire sauce

2 tbsp chopped fresh basil

fresh basil sprigs, to garnish

warm crusty bread, to serve

cook's tip

Most brands of Worcestershire sauce contain anchovies, so if you are a vegetarian, check the label to make sure you choose a vegetarian variety.

1 Cook the potato cubes in a saucepan of lightly salted boiling water for 7–8 minutes. Drain well and reserve.

2 Heat the olive oil in a large, heavy-based frying pan. Add the potato cubes and cook over a medium heat, stirring, for 8–10 minutes, until browned.

3 Add the crushed garlic and pepper cubes and cook, stirring frequently, for 2–3 minutes. Add the tomatoes and mushrooms and cook, stirring frequently, for 5–6 minutes.

4 Stir in the Worcestershire sauce and basil and season to taste with salt and pepper. Transfer to a warmed serving dish, garnish with basil leaves and serve with warm crusty bread.

sweet & sour vegetables

serves 4   **prep: 45 mins** ⏲   **cook: 30 mins** ⏲

This is a dish of Persian origin – not Chinese, as it sounds. Plump diced aubergines are fried and mixed with tomatoes, mint, sugar and vinegar to give a unique combination of flavours.

INGREDIENTS

2 large aubergines

salt and pepper

6 tbsp olive oil

4 garlic cloves, crushed

1 onion, cut into eighths

4 large tomatoes, deseeded and chopped

3 tbsp chopped fresh mint

150 ml/5 fl oz Vegetable Stock (see page 13)

4 tsp brown sugar

2 tbsp red wine vinegar

1 tsp chilli flakes

fresh mint sprigs, to garnish

NUTRITIONAL INFORMATION

Calories 218

Protein 3g

Carbohydrate 14g

Sugars 12g

Fat 17g

Saturates 3g

---

variation

Substitute 1 teaspoon of chopped fresh red chilli for the chilli flakes to give the dish a slightly milder flavour.

---

cook's tip

Choose firm, glossy aubergines for this dish. Large aubergines benefit from salting to extract their juices – small aubergines are less bitter, and can often be cooked without salting.

1 Cut the aubergines into cubes. Place them in a colander, sprinkle with plenty of salt and leave to stand for 30 minutes to remove all the bitter juices. Rinse thoroughly under cold running water and pat dry with kitchen paper.

2 Heat the oil in a large, heavy-based frying pan. Add the aubergine and cook over a medium heat, stirring, for 1–2 minutes, or until beginning to colour. Stir in the garlic and onion wedges and cook, stirring constantly, for a further 2–3 minutes.

3 Stir in the tomatoes, mint and stock. Reduce the heat, cover and simmer for 15–20 minutes, or until the aubergine is tender.

4 Add the brown sugar, red wine vinegar and chilli flakes, then season to taste with salt and pepper and cook for a further 2–3 minutes, stirring.

5 Transfer to a warmed serving dish, garnish with fresh mint sprigs and serve immediately.

vegetable chilli

cook: 1 hr 15 mins   **prep: 10 mins**   **serves 4**

variation

If you prefer a hotter dish, stir in a little extra chilli powder when you adjust the seasoning at the end of Step 4.

This is a hearty and flavoursome dish that works well served on its own, and is delicious spooned over cooked rice or baked potatoes to make a more substantial meal.

INGREDIENTS

1 aubergine, cut into 2.5-cm/1-inch slices

1 tbsp olive oil, plus extra for brushing

1 large red or yellow onion, finely chopped

2 red or yellow peppers, deseeded and finely chopped

3–4 garlic cloves, finely chopped or crushed

800 g/1 lb 12 oz canned chopped tomatoes

1 tbsp mild chilli powder

½ tsp ground cumin

½ tsp dried oregano

salt and pepper

2 small courgettes, quartered lengthways and sliced

400 g/14 oz canned kidney beans, drained and rinsed

450 ml/16 fl oz water

1 tbsp tomato purée

6 spring onions, finely chopped

115 g/4 oz Cheddar cheese, grated

cook's tip

If you would prefer to leave the purple aubergine skin out of this chilli, you can peel the aubergine before cutting it into slices.

1 Brush the aubergine slices on one side with oil. Heat half the oil in a large, heavy-based frying pan. Add the aubergine slices, oiled-side up, and cook over a medium heat for 5–6 minutes, or until browned on one side. Turn the slices over, cook on the other side until browned and transfer to a plate. Cut into bite-sized pieces.

2 Heat the remaining oil in a large saucepan over a medium heat. Add the chopped onion and peppers to the saucepan and cook, stirring occasionally, for 3–4 minutes, or until the onion is just softened, but not browned. Add the garlic and cook for a further 2–3 minutes, or until the onion just begins to colour.

3 Add the tomatoes, chilli powder, cumin and oregano. Season to taste with salt and pepper. Bring just to the boil, reduce the heat, cover and simmer gently for 15 minutes.

4 Add the sliced courgettes, aubergine pieces and kidney beans. Stir in the water and tomato purée. Return to the boil, then cover the saucepan and simmer for a further 45 minutes, or until the vegetables are tender. Taste and adjust the seasoning, if necessary.

5 Ladle into warmed bowls and top with spring onions and cheese.

vegetable curry

serves 4 **prep: 10 mins** ⏲ **cook: 45 mins** ⏲

This colourful and interesting mixture of vegetables, cooked in a spicy sauce, is excellent served with rice and naan bread.

INGREDIENTS

1 aubergine

225 g/8 oz turnips

350 g/12 oz new potatoes

225 g/8 oz cauliflower

225 g/8 oz button mushrooms

1 large onion

3 carrots

6 tbsp ghee

2 garlic cloves, crushed

4 tsp finely chopped fresh root ginger

1–2 fresh green chillies, deseeded and chopped

1 tbsp paprika

2 tsp ground coriander

1 tbsp mild or medium curry powder

450 ml/16 fl oz Vegetable Stock (see page 13)

400 g/14 oz canned chopped tomatoes

salt

1 green pepper, deseeded and sliced

1 tbsp cornflour

150 ml/5 fl oz coconut milk

2–3 tbsp ground almonds

fresh coriander sprigs, to garnish

freshly cooked rice, to serve

NUTRITIONAL INFORMATION

Calories 421

Protein 12g

Carbohydrate 42g

Sugars 20g

Fat 24g

Saturates 3g

---

variation

You can use vegetable oil instead of the ghee, and substitute peeled swede for the turnip, if you prefer.

---

cook's tip

Ghee is clarified butter, which contains no milk solids. It can be heated to much higher temperatures than ordinary butter. It is available from Indian food stores and large supermarkets.

1 Cut the aubergine, turnips and potatoes into 1-cm/½-inch cubes. Divide the cauliflower into small florets. Leave the button mushrooms whole or slice them thickly, if preferred. Slice the onion and carrots.

2 Heat the ghee in a large saucepan. Add the onion, turnip, potato and

cauliflower and cook over a low heat, stirring frequently, for 3 minutes.

3 Add the garlic, ginger, chillies, paprika, ground coriander and curry powder and cook, stirring, for 1 minute.

4 Add the stock, tomatoes, aubergine and mushrooms and season

with salt. Cover and simmer, stirring occasionally, for 30 minutes, or until tender. Add the green pepper and carrots, cover and cook for a further 5 minutes.

5 Place the cornflour and coconut milk in a bowl, combine into a smooth paste and stir into the vegetable mixture. Add the ground

almonds and simmer, stirring constantly, for 2 minutes. Taste and adjust the seasoning, if necessary. Transfer to serving plates, garnish with coriander sprigs and serve immediately with freshly cooked rice.

yellow curry

serves 4   **prep: 5 mins** ◔   **cook: 15 mins** ♨

Potatoes are not highly regarded in Thai cookery because rice is the traditional staple food, but this dish is a tasty exception.

INGREDIENTS

2 garlic cloves, finely chopped

3-cm/1¼-inch piece of galangal, finely chopped

1 lemon grass stalk, finely chopped

1 tsp coriander seeds

3 tbsp vegetable oil

2 tsp Thai red curry paste

½ tsp ground turmeric

200 ml/7 fl oz coconut milk

250 g/9 oz potatoes, cut into cubes

100 ml/3½ fl oz Vegetable Stock (see page 13)

200 g/7 oz fresh young spinach leaves

1 small onion, thinly sliced into rings

NUTRITIONAL INFORMATION

Calories	160
Protein	3g
Carbohydrate	15g
Sugars	4g
Fat	10g
Saturates	1g

cook's tip

Choose a firm, waxy potato for this dish, one that will keep its shape during cooking, in preference to a floury variety that will break up easily.

1 Put the garlic, galangal, lemon grass and coriander seeds into a mortar and crush with a pestle to make a smooth paste.

2 Heat 2 tablespoons of the oil in a large, heavy-based frying pan or preheated wok. Stir in the fresh garlic and spice paste and stir-fry over a high heat for 30 seconds, then stir in the curry paste and turmeric, add the coconut milk and bring to the boil.

3 Add the potatoes and stock. Return to the boil, then reduce the heat and simmer, uncovered, for 10–12 minutes, or until the potatoes are almost tender.

4 Stir in the spinach and simmer until the leaves have wilted.

5 Heat the remaining oil in a separate frying pan, add the onion and cook until crisp and golden brown. Place on top of the curry just before serving.

spiced cashew nut curry

⏱ **cook: 25 mins**   ⏱ **prep: 15 mins, plus 8 hrs soaking**   **serves 4**

This unusual vegetarian dish is best served as a side dish with other curries and with rice to soak up the wonderfully rich, spiced juices.

NUTRITIONAL INFORMATION

Calories 455

Protein 13g

Carbohydrate 16g

Sugars 6g

Fat 39g

Saturates 11g

INGREDIENTS

250 g/9 oz unsalted cashew nuts

1 small fresh green chilli

1 tsp coriander seeds

1 tsp cumin seeds

2 cardamom pods, crushed

1 tbsp sunflower oil

1 onion, thinly sliced

1 garlic clove, crushed

1 cinnamon stick

½ tsp ground turmeric

4 tbsp coconut cream

300 ml/10 fl oz hot Vegetable Stock
(see page 13)

3 kaffir lime leaves, finely shredded

freshly cooked jasmine rice, to serve

cook's tip

All spices give the best flavour when freshly crushed, but if you prefer, you can use ground spices instead of putting them into a mortar and crushing with a pestle.

1 Soak the cashew nuts in cold water for 8 hours, or overnight, then drain well. Deseed and chop the chilli. Put the coriander seeds, cumin seeds and cardamom pods into a mortar and crush with a pestle.

2 Heat the oil in a heavy-based frying pan and stir-fry the onion and garlic over a medium heat for 2–3 minutes to soften, but not brown. Add the chilli, crushed spices, cinnamon stick and turmeric and stir-fry for a further 1 minute.

3 Add the coconut cream and the hot stock to the frying pan. Bring to the boil, then add the cashew nuts and lime leaves.

Reduce the heat, cover and simmer for 20 minutes. Serve hot, accompanied by freshly cooked jasmine rice.

winter vegetable cobbler

cook: 40 mins   **prep: 20 mins**   **serves 4**

variation

Substitute broccoli florets for the cauliflower, or chopped turnips for the swede, if you prefer.

Seasonal fresh vegetables are casseroled with lentils then topped with a ring of fresh cheese scones to make this tasty cobbler.

INGREDIENTS

1 tbsp olive oil

1 garlic clove, crushed

8 small onions, halved

2 celery sticks, sliced

225 g/8 oz swede, chopped

2 carrots, sliced

½ small cauliflower, broken into florets

225 g/8 oz mushrooms, sliced

400 g/14 oz canned chopped tomatoes

55 g/2 oz red split lentils, rinsed

2 tbsp cornflour

3–4 tbsp water

300 ml/10 fl oz Vegetable Stock (see page 13)

2 tsp Tabasco sauce

2 tsp chopped fresh oregano

fresh oregano sprigs, to garnish

TOPPING

225 g/8 oz self-raising flour

pinch of salt

4 tbsp butter

115 g/4 oz mature Cheddar cheese, grated

2 tsp chopped fresh oregano

1 egg, lightly beaten

150 ml/5 fl oz milk

cook's tip

Use a scone cutter to cut out the dough rounds, to give the edges a decorative shape. When you arrange the scones around the dish, make sure that you overlap them slightly.

1 Preheat the oven to 180°C/350°F/Gas Mark 4. Heat the oil in a large frying pan and cook the garlic and onions over a low heat for 5 minutes. Add the celery, swede, carrots and cauliflower and cook for 2–3 minutes.

2 Add the mushrooms, tomatoes and lentils. Place the cornflour and water in a bowl and mix to make a smooth paste. Stir into the frying pan with the stock, Tabasco and oregano. Transfer to an ovenproof dish, cover and bake in the preheated oven for 20 minutes.

3 To make the topping, sift the flour and salt into a bowl. Rub in the butter, then stir in most of the cheese and the chopped oregano. Beat the egg with the milk in a small bowl and add enough to the dry ingredients to make a soft dough. Knead, then roll out to 1-cm/½-inch thick and cut into 5-cm/2-inch rounds.

4 Remove the dish from the oven and increase the temperature to 200°C/400°F/Gas Mark 6. Arrange the dough rounds around the edge of the dish, brush with the remaining egg and milk mixture and sprinkle with the reserved cheese. Cook for a further 10–12 minutes. Garnish with oregano sprigs and serve.

cauliflower bake

serves 4   **prep: 10 mins** ⏲   **cook: 40 mins** ⏱

The bright red of the tomatoes is a great contrast to the colours of the cauliflower and herbs in this dish, making it appealing to both the eye and the palate. It is easy to prepare and satisfying to eat.

INGREDIENTS

500 g/1 lb 2 oz cauliflower, broken into florets

600 g/1 lb 5 oz potatoes, cut into cubes

100 g/3½ oz cherry tomatoes

chopped fresh flat-leaved parsley, to garnish

SAUCE

25 g/1 oz butter or margarine

1 leek, sliced

1 garlic clove, crushed

3 tbsp plain flour

300 ml/10 fl oz milk

85 g/3 oz mixed cheese, such as Cheddar, Parmesan and Gruyère, grated

½ tsp paprika

2 tbsp chopped fresh flat-leaved parsley

salt and pepper

NUTRITIONAL INFORMATION

Calories 305

Protein 15g

Carbohydrate 31g

Sugars 9g

Fat 14g

Saturates . . . . .6 g

variation

You can use broccoli instead of cauliflower for this dish, if you prefer. Alternatively, use a mixture of broccoli and cauliflower for a mix of colours.

cook's tip

When you choose a fresh cauliflower for this dish, look for a tightly packed flower with no brown marks or blemishes, surrounded by plenty of protective leaves.

1 Preheat the oven to 180°C/350°F/Gas Mark 4. Cook the cauliflower florets in a saucepan of boiling water for 10 minutes. Meanwhile, cook the potatoes in a saucepan of boiling water for 10 minutes. Drain both vegetables and reserve.

2 To make the sauce, melt the butter in a large saucepan, add the leek and garlic and cook over a low heat for 1 minute. Stir in the flour and cook, stirring constantly, for 1 minute. Remove the saucepan from the heat, then gradually stir in the milk, 55 g/2 oz of the cheese, the paprika and parsley. Return the saucepan to the heat and bring to the boil, stirring constantly. Season to taste with salt and pepper.

3 Transfer the cauliflower to a deep ovenproof dish with the cherry tomatoes, and top with the potatoes. Pour the sauce over the potatoes and sprinkle over the remaining grated cheese.

4 Cook in the preheated oven for 20 minutes, or until the vegetables are cooked through and the cheese is golden brown and bubbling. Garnish with chopped parsley and serve immediately.

potato-topped vegetables

⏱ **cook: 1 hr 15 mins**   ⏱ **prep: 20 mins**   **serves 4**

This is a very colourful and nutritious dish, packed full of tasty, crunchy vegetables, coated in a creamy white wine sauce.

variation

You can parboil almost any selection of vegetables for this dish. Try stirring a handful of frozen peas into the vegetable mixture at the end of Step 2.

INGREDIENTS

1 carrot, diced

175 g/6 oz cauliflower florets

175 g/6 oz broccoli florets

1 fennel bulb, sliced

85 g/3 oz French beans, halved

25 g/1 oz butter

25 g/1 oz plain flour

150 ml/5 fl oz Vegetable Stock (see page 13)

150 ml/5 fl oz dry white wine

150 ml/5 fl oz milk

175 g/6 oz chestnut mushrooms, quartered

2 tbsp chopped fresh sage

TOPPING

900 g/2 lb floury potatoes, diced

25 g/1 oz butter

4 tbsp natural yogurt

70 g/2½ oz freshly grated Parmesan cheese

1 tsp fennel seeds

salt and pepper

cook's tip

For an extra creamy topping, mash the potatoes with the butter and yogurt in Step 3, and before mashing in the cheese, beat the mixture for 1–2 minutes with a hand-held whisk.

1 Preheat the oven to 190°C/375°F/Gas Mark 5. Cook the carrot, cauliflower, broccoli, fennel and beans in a saucepan of boiling water for 10 minutes until just tender. Drain the vegetables and reserve.

2 Melt the butter in a saucepan. Stir in the flour and cook over a low heat for 1 minute. Remove from the heat and stir in the stock, wine and milk. Return to the heat and bring to the boil, stirring, until thickened. Stir in the reserved vegetables, mushrooms and chopped sage.

3 To make the topping, cook the potatoes in a saucepan of boiling water for 10–15 minutes. Drain and mash with the butter, yogurt and half the cheese. Stir in the fennel seeds. Season to taste.

4 Spoon the vegetable mixture into a 1-litre/1¾-pint pie dish. Spoon the potato mixture over the top, sprinkle over the remaining cheese and cook in the oven for 30–35 minutes, or until golden. Serve immediately.

rice & pasta

A staple for half the world, rice is one of the most versatile of ingredients, partnering vegetables, meat, poultry, fish and shellfish with equal ease. From the United States to Thailand, almost every country in the world has its own favourite rice-based dish. Most famous of all, perhaps, are Italy's risottos, and this chapter features three, very different but absolutely delicious versions, with hints and tips on how to achieve the desired creamy perfection.

Pasta and noodles also play an important role in the cuisines of the world – but most are not one-pot dishes. As a general rule, pasta and sauce are cooked separately and, although recipes may be easy, there is no getting away from using several saucepans. Well, the exception proves the rule and this chapter includes the fabulous Pasta with Garlic & Pine Kernels (see page 149), with its delicious no-cook sauce, and the scrumptious all-in-one Crisp Noodle & Vegetable Stir-fry (see page 150).

Some dishes are flavoured with meat or fish, others are vegetarian or even vegan. Delight your guests with saffron-coloured Spanish Rice with Chicken (see page 135), a mouthwatering Jambalaya (see page 140) or a luxuriously rich-tasting Risotto with Four Cheeses (see page 144). If you are in a hurry for the family supper, why not try Pork Hash (see page 138) or Pasta with Pesto (see page 152) and, if it's too hot to do much cooking, then Tricolour Pasta Salad (see page 148) is an almost instant solution.

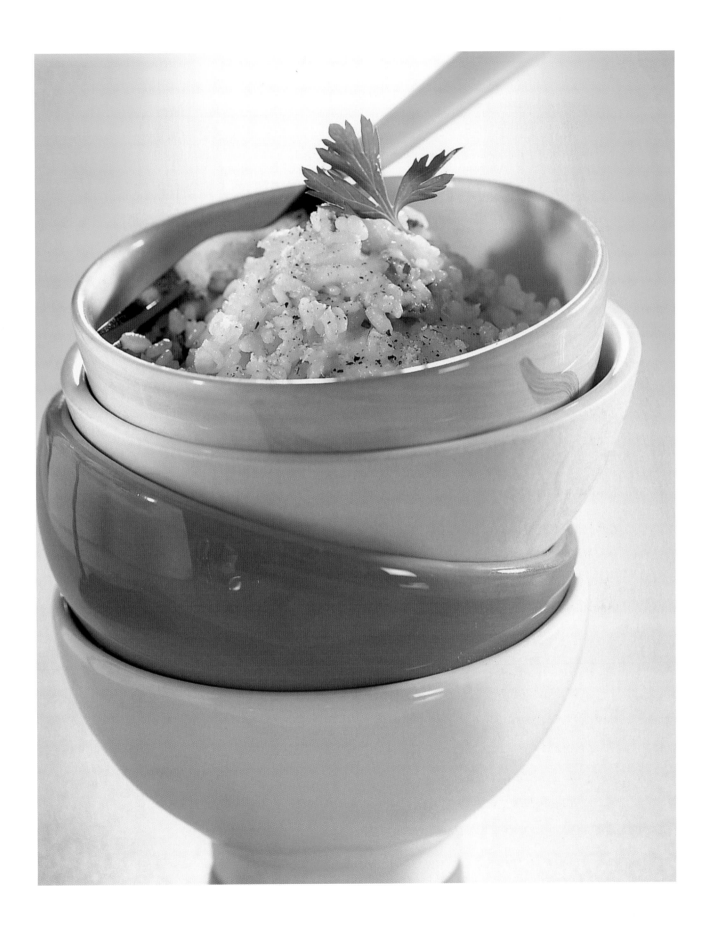

greek chicken & rice

serves 4 | **prep: 15 mins** | **cook: 40–45 mins**

Look for large, slightly wrinkled Greek olives marinated in oil, and for ewe's milk feta cheese, to give this dish an authentic flavour.

INGREDIENTS

8 chicken thighs

2 tbsp sunflower oil

1 onion, chopped

2 garlic cloves, finely chopped

175 g/6 oz long-grain rice

225 ml/8 fl oz Chicken Stock
(see page 13)

800 g/1 lb 12 oz canned
chopped tomatoes

1 tbsp chopped fresh thyme

2 tbsp chopped fresh oregano

12 black olives, stoned and chopped

55 g/2 oz feta cheese, crumbled

fresh oregano sprigs, to garnish

NUTRITIONAL INFORMATION

Calories 417

Protein 25g

Carbohydrate 47g

Sugars 8g

Fat 16g

Saturates 3g

cook's tip

If you can afford organic chicken, it will have a better texture and flavour than ordinary chicken. If you are using frozen chicken, check that it is thoroughly thawed before you begin cooking.

1 Remove the skin from the chicken. Heat the oil in a flameproof casserole. Add the chicken, in batches, if necessary, and cook over a medium heat, turning occasionally, for 8–10 minutes, or until golden. Transfer to a plate with a slotted spoon.

2 Add the onion, garlic, long-grain rice and about 50 ml/2 fl oz of the stock to the casserole and cook, stirring, for 5 minutes, or until the onion is softened. Pour in the remaining stock and add the tomatoes and their juices and the herbs.

3 Return the chicken thighs to the casserole, pushing them down into the rice. Bring to the boil, then reduce the heat, cover and simmer for 25–30 minutes, or until the chicken is cooked through and tender. Stir in the olives and sprinkle the cheese on top. Garnish with oregano sprigs and serve immediately.

spanish rice with chicken

⏱ **cook: 1 hr 10 mins**   ⏱ **prep: 15 mins**   **serves 4**

Saffron gives this hearty, warming dish a lovely sunshine-yellow colour, while mild green chillies add a kick to the flavour.

NUTRITIONAL INFORMATION

Calories	.616
Protein	.52g
Carbohydrate	.47g
Sugars	.7g
Fat	.24g
Saturates	.5g

INGREDIENTS

3 tbsp olive oil

1.25 kg/2 lb 12 oz chicken pieces

salt and pepper

2 onions, sliced

175 g/6 oz long-grain rice

125 ml/4 fl oz dry white wine

pinch of saffron threads, lightly crushed

350 ml/12 fl oz Chicken Stock

(see page 13)

1–2 mild fresh green chillies,

such as serrano

2 garlic cloves, finely chopped

2 beef tomatoes, peeled, deseeded

and chopped

fresh coriander sprigs, to garnish

variation

For extra colour, garnish the dish with 140 g/5 oz of bottled pimientos – a mild variety of pepper – cut into very thin strips.

1 Heat 2 tablespoons of the oil in a flameproof casserole. Season the chicken, add to the casserole and cook over a medium heat, turning occasionally, for 8–10 minutes, or until golden. Transfer to a plate with a slotted spoon.

2 Add the remaining oil to the casserole. Add the onions and cook over a low heat, stirring occasionally, for 5 minutes, or until translucent. Add the rice and cook, stirring, for 2 minutes, or until the grains are transparent and coated with oil.

3 Pour in the wine. Bring to the boil, then reduce the heat, cover and simmer for 8 minutes, or until all the liquid has been absorbed. Combine the saffron and stock and pour into the casserole. Stir in the chillies and garlic and season to taste with salt. Cover and simmer for 15 minutes.

4 Add the tomatoes and return the chicken pieces to the casserole, pushing them down into the rice. Cover and cook for a further 25 minutes, or until the chicken is cooked through and tender. Garnish with coriander sprigs and serve.

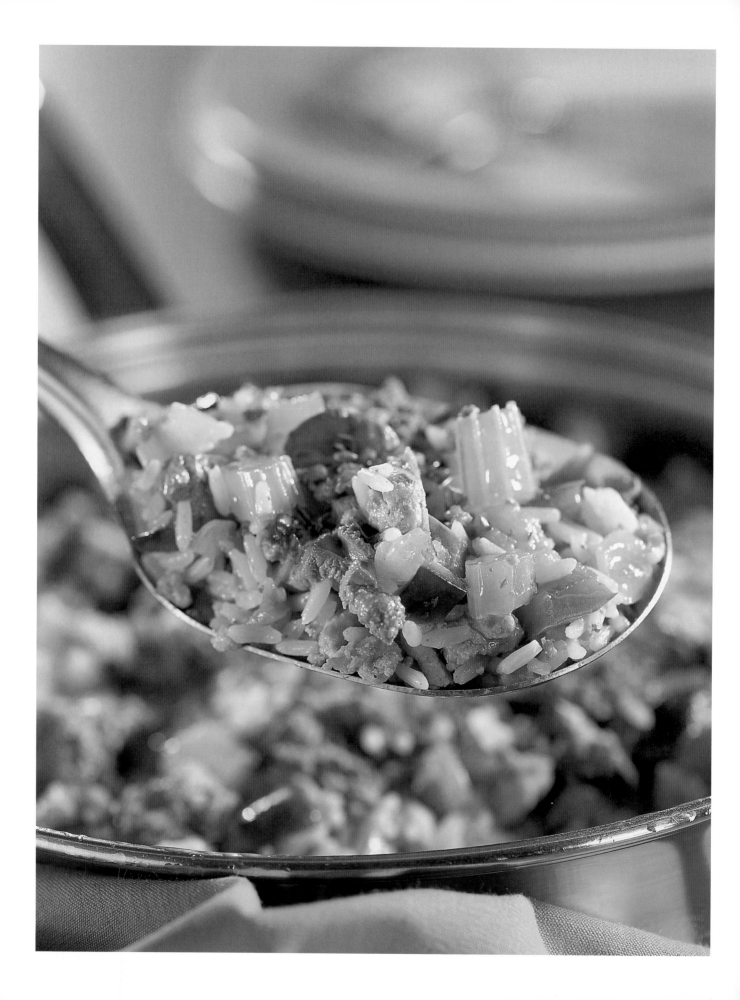

louisiana rice

cook: 30 mins

prep: 20 mins, plus 15 mins standing

serves 4

This lightly spiced, filling dish from the Deep South of America is quick, easy and economical – perfect for a midweek supper.

NUTRITIONAL INFORMATION

Calories	394
Protein	. . . . .26g
Carbohydrate	. . . . .36g
Sugars	. . . . .5g
Fat	. . . . .17g
Saturates	. . . . .3g

variation

You can substitute a small courgette, chopped, for the celery, if you would prefer a milder flavour in this dish.

INGREDIENTS

4 tbsp sunflower or corn oil

225 g/8 oz fresh pork mince

1 onion, chopped

1 garlic clove, finely chopped

1 aubergine, diced

1 green pepper, deseeded and diced

2 celery sticks, chopped

1 tsp paprika

1 tsp cayenne pepper

1 tbsp chopped fresh thyme

salt and pepper

425 ml/15 fl oz Chicken Stock (see page 13)

225 g/8 oz chicken livers, minced

140 g/5 oz long-grain rice

1 bay leaf

3 tbsp chopped fresh parsley

cook's tip

Rinsing uncooked rice in cold water helps to remove some of the starch. This ensures that the grains are less likely to stick together during cooking.

1 Heat the oil in a large, heavy-based frying pan. Add the pork and cook over a medium heat, stirring, for 8–10 minutes, or until broken up and browned all over.

2 Add the onion, garlic, aubergine, green pepper, celery, paprika, cayenne and thyme and season to taste with salt and pepper.

Cover and cook, stirring frequently, for 5 minutes. Stir in the stock, scraping up any sediment on the base of the frying pan. Cover and simmer for 5 minutes.

3 Add the chicken livers and cook for 2–3 minutes. Stir in the rice and the bay leaf. Cover and simmer for 7 minutes, then remove the

frying pan from the heat, but do not uncover. Leave to steam for 15 minutes, or until the rice is tender. Stir in the parsley, fluff up the rice and serve immediately.

pork hash

serves 4   **prep: 10 mins** ⏲   **cook: 55 mins** ⏱

This is a tasty dish for a midweek supper – once it's in the oven, you can put your feet up, relax with a glass of wine, and look forward to a filling meal with a feast of flavours.

INGREDIENTS

400 g/14 oz canned chopped tomatoes

600–700 ml/1–1¼ pints Beef Stock
(see page 13)

1 tbsp sunflower oil

450 g/1 lb fresh pork mince

1 large onion, chopped

1 red pepper, deseeded and chopped

400 g/14 oz long-grain rice

1 tbsp chilli powder

450 g/1 lb fresh or frozen green beans

salt and pepper

NUTRITIONAL INFORMATION

Calories 625

Protein 34g

Carbohydrate 100g

Sugars 11g

Fat 13g

Saturates 3g

variation

For a beef hash, substitute beef mince for the pork, and if you prefer, use peas instead of beans.

1 Preheat the oven to 180°C/350°F/Gas Mark 4. Drain the tomatoes, reserving their juices, and reserve. Make the juices up to 850 ml/1½ pints with the stock and reserve.

2 Heat the oil in a large, flameproof casserole. Add the pork, onion and red pepper and cook over a medium heat, stirring frequently, for 8–10 minutes, or until the onion is softened and the meat is broken up and golden brown. Add the rice and cook, stirring constantly, for 2 minutes.

3 Add the tomatoes, stock mixture, chilli powder and beans to the casserole and season to taste with salt and pepper. Bring to the boil, then cover and transfer to the preheated oven to bake for 40 minutes. Serve immediately.

tuna rice

⏲ **cook: 10 mins**   ⏱ **prep: 10 mins**   **serves 4**

This is a scrumptious way to use up leftover boiled rice. Alternatively, next time you are serving rice with a meal, cook an extra 250 g/9 oz and serve this easy dish the next day.

NUTRITIONAL INFORMATION	
Calories 460	
Protein 20g	
Carbohydrate 66g	
Sugars 1g	
Fat 14g	
Saturates 2g	

INGREDIENTS

3 tbsp groundnut or sunflower oil

4 spring onions, chopped

2 garlic cloves, finely chopped

200 g/7 oz canned tuna in oil, drained and flaked

175 g/6 oz frozen or canned sweetcorn kernels and peppers

750 g/1 lb 10 oz cold boiled rice

2 tbsp Thai fish sauce

1 tbsp light soy sauce

salt and pepper

2 tbsp chopped fresh coriander, to garnish

cook's tip

Leftover cooked rice should be cooled quickly, stored in the refrigerator and eaten within 24 hours. It is essential that the rice is cold and dry before you stir-fry it, otherwise it will become sticky.

1 Heat the groundnut oil in a preheated wok or large, heavy-based frying pan. Add the spring onions and stir-fry for 2 minutes, then add the garlic and stir-fry for a further 1 minute.

2 Add the tuna and the sweetcorn and peppers, and stir-fry for 2 minutes.

3 Add the rice, fish sauce and soy sauce and stir-fry for 2 minutes. Season to taste with salt and pepper and serve immediately, garnished with chopped coriander.

jambalaya

serves 6   **prep: 20 mins**   **cook: 50–55 mins**

This Cajun dish is borrowed from Spain, where it originated. Its lively mixture of chicken and prawns makes it a good dish to serve at a brunch party, instead of the more traditional kedgeree.

INGREDIENTS

2 tbsp lard	12 Mediterranean prawns, peeled
1.5 kg/3 lb 5 oz chicken pieces	225 g/8 oz long-grain rice
25 g/1 oz plain flour	450 ml/16 fl oz Chicken Stock
225 g/8 oz rindless smoked	(see page 13) or water
gammon, diced	dash of Tabasco sauce
1 onion, chopped	salt and pepper
1 orange pepper, deseeded and sliced	3 spring onions, finely chopped
350 g/12 oz tomatoes, peeled	2 tbsp chopped fresh
and chopped	flat-leaved parsley
1 garlic clove, finely chopped	fresh flat-leaved parsley sprigs,
1 tsp chopped fresh thyme	to garnish

NUTRITIONAL INFORMATION

Calories	.570
Protein	.59g
Carbohydrate	.42g
Sugars	.3g
Fat	.20g
Saturates	.5g

variation

If you don't want to use lard in this recipe, substitute 2 tablespoons of corn oil at the beginning of Step 1.

cook's tip

Jambalaya is a Cajun dish, the idea for which originally came from Spain. If you like an even hotter taste, add 1 teaspoon of cayenne pepper with the seasoning in Step 3.

1 Melt the lard in a large, flameproof casserole. Add the chicken and cook over a medium heat, turning occasionally, for 8–10 minutes, or until golden brown all over. Transfer the chicken to a plate with a slotted spoon.

2 Add the flour and cook over a very low heat, stirring, for 15 minutes, or until golden brown. Do not let it burn. Return the chicken pieces to the casserole with the gammon, onion, orange pepper, tomatoes, garlic and thyme. Cook, stirring frequently, for 10 minutes.

3 Stir in the prawns, rice and stock and season to taste with Tabasco, salt and pepper. Bring the mixture to the boil, reduce the heat and cook for 15–20 minutes, or until all of the liquid has been absorbed and the rice is tender. Stir in the spring onions and chopped parsley, garnish with parsley sprigs and serve immediately.

seafood risotto

cook: 30 mins   **prep: 15 mins**   **serves 4**

NUTRITIONAL INFORMATION

Calories 547

Protein 46g

Carbohydrate 60g

Sugars 8g

Fat 15g

Saturates 6g

variation

You can substitute chunks of monkfish
for the cod to give the dish a slightly
meatier texture, if you prefer.

*The secret of a successful risotto is to use round grain Italian rice,
such as arborio, and to add a ladleful of stock at a time, making
sure that it is fully absorbed before more is added.*

INGREDIENTS

350 g/12 oz skinless cod fillet

25 g/1 oz unsalted butter

1 onion, chopped

2 red peppers, deseeded and chopped

4 tomatoes, peeled, deseeded
and chopped

8 ready-prepared scallops

2 tbsp olive oil

225 g/8 oz risotto rice

450 ml/16 fl oz hot Fish Stock
(see page 13)

salt

225 g/8 oz cooked peeled prawns

1 tbsp chopped flat-leaved parsley

2 tbsp freshly grated Parmesan cheese

fresh parsley sprigs, to garnish

cook's tip

Risotto rice will absorb stock
more readily if the stock is
kept at simmering point in
another saucepan while it is
being added in Step 2.

1 Cut the fish into cubes.
Melt half the butter
in a large saucepan. Add
the onion, red peppers and
tomatoes and cook over a low
heat, stirring occasionally, for
5 minutes, or until softened.
Add the fish and scallops, and
cook for a further 3 minutes.
Transfer the fish mixture to a
plate with a slotted spoon,
cover and reserve.

2 Add the oil to the pan
and heat gently. Add
the rice and stir to coat with
the butter and oil. Stir in a
ladleful of stock and season to
taste with salt. Cook, stirring,
until the stock has been
absorbed. Continue cooking
and adding stock, a ladleful at
a time, for 20 minutes, or until
the rice is tender and all of the
liquid has been absorbed.

3 Gently stir in the
reserved fish mixture
with the prawns and heat
through for 2 minutes.
Transfer the risotto to a
warmed serving dish, sprinkle
with the chopped parsley and
Parmesan cheese and serve
immediately, garnished with
parsley sprigs.

risotto with four cheeses

serves 4 **prep: 15 mins** **cook: 30 mins**

Rich and with a subtle flavour, this is a classic Italian dish that would normally be served before the main course.

INGREDIENTS

55 g/2 oz Taleggio cheese

55 g/2 oz Fontina cheese

55 g/2 oz Parmesan cheese

55 g/2 oz Gorgonzola cheese

40 g/1½ oz unsalted butter

1 onion, finely chopped

350 g/12 oz risotto rice

200 ml/7 fl oz dry white wine

1 litre/1¾ pints hot Vegetable Stock

(see page 13)

salt and pepper

fresh flat-leaved parsley sprigs,

to garnish

NUTRITIONAL INFORMATION

Calories	.425
Protein	.14g
Carbohydrate	.53g
Sugars	.2g
Fat	.17g
Saturates	.11g

variation

You can use other cheeses for this risotto, but try to get a mixture of flavours. Try a combination of dolcelatte, Gruyère, buffalo mozzarella and pecorino.

1 Grate the Taleggio, Fontina and Parmesan cheeses and crumble the Gorgonzola cheese, then reserve until required.

2 Melt the butter in a large saucepan, add the onion and cook over a low heat, stirring occasionally, for 5 minutes, or until softened. Add the rice and stir to coat the grains with butter. Add the wine and cook until almost all of it has been absorbed.

3 Add a ladleful of stock and cook, stirring, until the liquid has been absorbed. Continue cooking and adding the stock, a ladleful at a time, for 20 minutes, or until the rice is tender and all of the liquid has been absorbed.

4 Turn off the heat and stir in the Gorgonzola, Taleggio, Fontina and one-quarter of the Parmesan cheese, until melted. Season to taste with salt and pepper. Transfer the risotto to a serving dish, sprinkle with the remaining Parmesan cheese, garnish with parsley sprigs and serve immediately.

risotto primavera

⏲ **cook: 30 mins**   ◔ **prep: 10 mins**   **serves 4**

As evenings get longer, the days grow warmer and the first spring vegetables ripen, this is the ideal choice for a midweek supper.

NUTRITIONAL INFORMATION

Calories 399

Protein 11g

Carbohydrate 54g

Sugars 4g

Fat 16g

Saturates 7g

INGREDIENTS

115 g/4 oz asparagus spears, cut into short lengths

2 young carrots, thinly sliced

25 g/1 oz unsalted butter

2 tbsp olive oil

1 white onion, chopped

2 garlic cloves, finely chopped

225 g/8 oz risotto rice

3 tbsp dry white wine

1 litre/1¾ pints hot Vegetable Stock (see page 13)

55 g/2 oz button mushrooms, halved

salt and pepper

55 g/2 oz freshly grated Parmesan cheese, to serve

cook's tip

White onions, which are very popular in Italy, are sweeter and milder than brown onions. Alternatively, you could use a red onion for this dish.

1 Blanch the asparagus and carrots in a large saucepan of boiling water and drain well.

2 Melt the butter with the oil in a large, heavy-based saucepan. Add the onion and garlic and cook over a low heat, stirring occasionally, for 5 minutes, or until softened. Add the

rice and stir well to coat the grains with the butter and oil mixture. Add the white wine and cook until the liquid has been fully absorbed.

3 Add a ladleful of stock to the rice and cook, stirring, until the liquid has been absorbed. Continue cooking and adding the stock, a ladleful at a time, for

20 minutes, or until the rice is tender and all of the liquid has been absorbed.

4 Gently stir in the asparagus, carrots and mushrooms, season to taste with salt and pepper and cook for a further 2 minutes, or until heated through. Serve immediately, handing the Parmesan cheese separately.

rice & peas

serves 4   **prep: 15 mins** ⟁   **cook: 30 mins** ⟁

This is a famous dish from the Veneto region of Italy, known as Risi e Bisi. Pancetta is cured belly of pork – this is the Italian equivalent of unsmoked bacon, and it is available from some large supermarkets and from Italian delicatessens.

INGREDIENTS

55 g/2 oz unsalted butter

1 tbsp olive oil

1 red onion, chopped

1 garlic clove, finely chopped

55 g/2 oz pancetta, chopped

1.4 litres/2½ pints Chicken Stock (see page 13)

250 g/9 oz fresh peas

salt and pepper

200 g/7 oz risotto rice

3 tbsp chopped fresh flat-leaved parsley

55 g/2 oz Parmesan cheese

Parmesan cheese shavings, to garnish

NUTRITIONAL INFORMATION

Calories 484

Protein 15g

Carbohydrate 52g

Sugars 4g

Fat 25g

Saturates 13g

variation

To use frozen peas, add them with the parsley in Step 3, but before adding the butter and cheese, cook for 5 minutes, until tender.

cook's tip

Try to use fresh rather than frozen peas for this recipe if at all possible. Much of the charm of the dish comes from their tenderness and freshness.

1 Melt half the butter with the olive oil in a large, heavy-based saucepan. Add the onion, garlic and pancetta and cook over a low heat, stirring occasionally, for 5 minutes, or until the onion has softened.

2 Add the stock and peas and season to taste with salt and pepper. Bring the mixture to the boil. Add the rice, return to the boil, then reduce the heat and simmer, stirring occasionally, for 20 minutes, or until the rice is tender.

3 Meanwhile, grate the Parmesan cheese and reserve until required. Add the parsley to the saucepan and stir in the remaining butter and the freshly grated Parmesan cheese. When the cheese has melted, transfer to a warmed dish, garnish with the Parmesan cheese shavings and serve immediately.

tricolour pasta salad

serves 4 | **prep: 10 mins** | **cook: 8–10 mins**

This prettily coloured salad is full of lovely refreshing flavours – tomatoes, cheese, avocado, basil and pine kernels.

INGREDIENTS

salt and pepper

175 g/6 oz dried fusilli

1 avocado

6 tomatoes, thinly sliced

225 g/8 oz mozzarella cheese, thinly sliced

2 tbsp toasted pine kernels

fresh basil leaves, to garnish

DRESSING

6 tbsp extra virgin olive oil

2 tbsp white wine vinegar

1 tsp Dijon mustard

2 tbsp shredded fresh basil leaves

pinch of sugar

NUTRITIONAL INFORMATION

Calories	593
Protein	. . . . .22g
Carbohydrate	. . . . .39g
Sugars	. . . . .7g
Fat	. . . . .40g
Saturates	. . . . .12g

cook's tip

Do not peel the avocado in advance of preparing and serving the salad, because the flesh quickly discolours on exposure to the air.

1 Bring a large saucepan of lightly salted water to the boil. Add the pasta, return to the boil and cook for 8–10 minutes, or until tender but still firm to the bite. Drain, refresh under cold running water and drain again.

2 To make the dressing, whisk the oil, vinegar, mustard, basil and sugar together in a small bowl until combined. Season to taste with salt and pepper.

3 Cut the avocado in half and remove the stone. Peel, then thinly slice the flesh lengthways.

4 Arrange the slices of avocado, tomato and mozzarella cheese, overlapping slightly, around the outside of a large serving platter. Add half the dressing to the pasta, toss well, then spoon into the centre of the platter. Pour the remaining dressing over the salad, sprinkle with the pine kernels, garnish with basil leaves and serve.

pasta with garlic & pine kernels

⏲ **cook: 10 mins**   ◔ **prep: 10 mins**   **serves 4**

When you are in a hurry, pasta is the answer. This tasty sauce can be prepared while the pasta is cooking to make a meal in minutes.

NUTRITIONAL INFORMATION

Calories 397

Protein 10g

Carbohydrate 48g

Sugars 3g

Fat 20g

Saturates 2g

INGREDIENTS

salt and pepper

250 g/9 oz dried elicoidali or penne

3 garlic cloves, roughly chopped

2 canned anchovy fillets, drained
and roughly chopped

2 tbsp bottled capers, drained
and finely chopped

1 tsp tarragon mustard

50 ml/2 fl oz extra virgin olive oil

4 tbsp chopped mixed fresh herbs,
such as tarragon, chives and
flat-leaved parsley

55 g/2 oz toasted pine kernels

1 tbsp lemon juice

Parmesan cheese shavings, to garnish

cook's tip

Time the pasta from the moment when the water returns to the boil and begin testing when it has been boiling for 8 minutes. Test by breaking off a small piece and biting it with your front teeth.

1 Bring a large saucepan of lightly salted water to the boil. Add the pasta, return to the boil and cook for 8–10 minutes, or until tender but still firm to the bite.

2 Meanwhile, put the garlic and anchovies into a mortar and pound with a pestle to make a paste. Scrape the paste into a bowl and stir in the capers and tarragon mustard.

3 Gradually stir in the oil, then add the chopped fresh herbs, toasted pine kernels and lemon juice and season the mixture to taste with salt and pepper.

4 Drain the pasta thoroughly and return it to the saucepan. Add the sauce and toss well to coat the pasta. Serve immediately, garnished with Parmesan cheese shavings.

crisp noodle & vegetable stir-fry

serves 4   **prep: 5 mins** ⏲   **cook: 15–20 mins** ⏲

*Once you have chopped the vegetables, this dish is quick and easy
to put together, and makes an attractive and nutritious meal for the
family, or for visitors expecting a bite to eat.*

INGREDIENTS

groundnut or sunflower oil,
for deep-frying

115 g/4 oz rice vermicelli,
broken into 7.5-cm/3-inch lengths

115 g/4 oz green beans,
cut into short lengths

2 carrots, cut into thin batons

2 courgettes, cut into thin batons

115 g/4 oz shiitake mushrooms, sliced

2.5-cm/1-inch piece fresh root
ginger, shredded

½ small head Chinese leaves, shredded

4 spring onions, shredded

85 g/3 oz beansprouts

2 tbsp dark soy sauce

2 tbsp Chinese rice wine

large pinch of sugar

2 tbsp roughly chopped fresh coriander

NUTRITIONAL INFORMATION

Calories 240

Protein 7g

Carbohydrate 33g

Sugars 6g

Fat 9g

Saturates 1g

---

variation

For a spicier version of this dish, add
1 deseeded and sliced fresh red chilli
with the shredded ginger in Step 2.

---

cook's tip

This dish also looks attractive
if you serve the noodles in
a small nest on top of the
stir-fried vegetables, rather
than tossing them with the
vegetables in Step 3.

1 Half-fill a preheated
wok or deep, heavy-
based frying pan with oil. Heat
to 180–190°C/350–375°F, or
until a cube of bread browns
in 30 seconds. Add the
noodles, in batches, and cook
for 1½–2 minutes, or until crisp
and puffed up. Remove and
drain on kitchen paper. Pour
off all but 2 tablespoons of oil
from the wok.

2 Heat the remaining oil
over a high heat, then
add the green beans and stir-
fry for 2 minutes. Add the
carrot and courgette batons,
sliced mushrooms and ginger
and stir-fry for a further
2 minutes. Add the shredded
Chinese leaves and spring
onions with the beansprouts
and stir-fry for a further
1 minute.

3 Add the soy sauce,
Chinese rice wine and
sugar and cook, stirring
constantly, for 1 minute. Add
the noodles and chopped
coriander and toss well.
Serve immediately.

pasta with pesto

serves 4   **prep: 10–15 mins**   **cook: 8–10 mins**

Traditionally, the Genoese make this delicious sauce with a pestle and mortar. The taste of this fresh pesto will be a revelation.

INGREDIENTS

salt

450 g/1 lb dried tagliatelle

fresh basil sprigs, to garnish

PESTO

2 garlic cloves

25 g/1 oz pine kernels

sea salt

115 g/4 oz fresh basil leaves

125 ml/4 fl oz olive oil

55 g/2 oz freshly grated

Parmesan cheese

NUTRITIONAL INFORMATION

Calories	.705
Protein	.21g
Carbohydrate	.85g
Sugars	.4g
Fat	.34g
Saturates	.6g

cook's tip

To store pesto, place it in a screw-top jar, cover the surface with a layer of olive oil and keep in the refrigerator for up to 1 month.

1 To make the pesto, place the garlic, pine kernels and a large pinch of sea salt in a blender or food processor and process briefly. Add the basil leaves and process to a paste.

2 With the motor running, gradually add the oil. Scrape into a bowl and beat in the cheese. Season to taste with salt. Alternatively, put the garlic, pine kernels, a large pinch of sea salt and basil leaves into a mortar and crush with a pestle to make a paste. Transfer to a bowl, work in the Parmesan cheese, then gradually add the oil, beating with a wooden spoon. Season to taste with salt.

3 Bring a large saucepan of lightly salted water to the boil. Add the pasta, return to the boil and cook for 8–10 minutes, or until tender but still firm to the bite. Drain well, return to the saucepan and toss with half the pesto, then divide between warmed serving plates and top with the remaining pesto. Garnish with basil sprigs and serve.

linguine with tomato sauce

 cook: 10 mins

 prep: 10 mins,
 plus 30 mins marinating

serves 4

The best time to cook this dish is in the middle of summer – you should use large, sun-ripened tomatoes for the fabulous fresh sauce.

NUTRITIONAL INFORMATION

Calories 683

Protein 15g

Carbohydrate 88g

Sugars 8g

Fat 33g

Saturates 4g

INGREDIENTS

4 large tomatoes, peeled,
deseeded and diced

2 garlic cloves, finely chopped

8 fresh basil leaves, shredded

1 tbsp chopped fresh parsley

1 tbsp chopped fresh oregano

150 ml/5 fl oz extra virgin olive oil

salt and pepper

450 g/1 lb dried linguine

115 g/4 oz stoned black olives, chopped

TO SERVE

baby lamb's lettuce

shredded beetroot

variation

You can serve any long pasta, such as spaghetti, with this sauce. If you use fresh pasta, cook for only 2–3 minutes after the water returns to the boil.

1 Place the tomatoes in a shallow, non-metallic dish. Add the garlic, basil, parsley, oregano and oil and season to taste with salt and pepper. Mix well, cover with clingfilm and leave to marinate for 30 minutes.

2 Bring a large saucepan of lightly salted water to the boil. Add the pasta, return to the boil and cook for 8–10 minutes, or until tender but still firm to the bite. Drain the pasta and return it to the saucepan.

3 Add the tomatoes with their marinade and the olives. Toss well and serve with baby lamb's lettuce and shredded beetroot.

desserts

For many cooks, dessert is one course too far, but for many diners, it is a fine finale to a meal. Compromise with this delightful selection of one-pot sweet dishes. Why bother with a conventional – and boring – fruit pie when, with far less effort and washing-up, you could make Clafoutis (see page 165), a melt-in-the-mouth combination of succulent cherries and crispy batter, or Tarte Tatin (see page 156), an all-in-one upside-down apple pie?

Whatever the season and whatever the occasion, you will find the perfect dish to round off your meal – whether an alfresco lunch, a midwinter supper or a sophisticated dinner party. There are lots of child-friendly treats for family suppers, from Pancake Pieces (see page 166) to Apple Fritters (see page 171), as well as some delicious dishes for the more adult palate, from Syllabub (see page 162) to liqueur-laced Saucy Ice Creams (see page 172). Fruit features in many forms – hot Flambéed Peaches (see page 163) contrast with ice-cold Forest Fruits Granita (see page 169), with Warm Fruit Compote (see page 164) somewhere in between.

There are also recipes for traditional, familiar and well-loved desserts, such as Creamed Rice Pudding (see page 159) and Zabaglione (see page 160). There are light-as-air confections and substantial puddings, to make sure that even the heartiest appetite is finally satisfied.

tarte tatin

serves 8 **prep: 15 mins,** ⟲ **cook: 1 hr 5 mins** ⟳
plus 10 mins cooling

This upside-down apple tart has been a speciality of Sologne in the Loire valley for centuries, but was made famous by the Tatin sisters who ran a hotel-restaurant in Lamotte-Beuvron at the beginning of the twentieth century.

INGREDIENTS

225 g/8 oz shortcrust pastry, thawed if frozen

plain flour, for dusting

10 eating apples, such as Golden Delicious

4 tbsp lemon juice

115 g/4 oz unsalted butter, diced

115 g/4 oz caster sugar

½ tsp ground cinnamon

NUTRITIONAL INFORMATION

Calories 348

Protein 2g

Carbohydrate 43g

Sugars 30g

Fat 20g

Saturates 11g

---

variation

If you can't find any Golden Delicious apples, Cox's apples will work just as well for this traditional French tart.

---

cook's tip

To achieve the best decorative effect when the tart is turned over, pack the halved apples in the tin with their cut sides facing up in Step 3.

---

1 Preheat the oven to 230°C/450°F/Gas Mark 8. Roll out the pastry on a lightly floured work surface into a 5-mm/¼-inch thick round, about 28 cm/11 inches in diameter. Transfer to a lightly floured baking tray and leave to chill in the refrigerator.

2 Peel, halve and core the apples, then brush with the lemon juice to prevent any discoloration. Heat the butter, sugar and cinnamon in a 25-cm/10-inch tarte tatin tin or heavy-based frying pan with a flameproof handle over a low heat, stirring occasionally, until the butter has melted and the sugar has dissolved. Cook for a further 6–8 minutes, or until the mixture is a light caramel colour. Remove from the heat.

3 Arrange the apples in the tin or frying pan, packing them in tightly. Return to the heat and cook for 25 minutes, or until the apples are tender and lightly coloured. Remove from the heat and leave to cool slightly.

4 Place the pastry over the apples, tucking in the edges. Prick the top and bake in the preheated oven for 30 minutes, or until golden. Leave to cool slightly, then run a knife around the edge of the tin to loosen the pastry. Invert on to a plate and serve warm.

teacup pudding

serves 4   **prep: 10 mins**   **cook: 3 hrs**

This is such an easy dessert to make, because all the ingredients, except the mixed spice, can be measured in the same cup. It tastes best served with a generous helping of warmed custard.

INGREDIENTS

butter, for greasing
1 cup self-raising flour
1 tsp mixed spice
1 cup soft brown sugar
1 cup shredded suet
1 cup currants
1 cup milk
custard, to serve

NUTRITIONAL INFORMATION

Calories . . . . .517 (per portion)

Protein 5g

Carbohydrate 72g

Sugars 46g

Fat 25g

Saturates 14g

cook's tip

It doesn't matter whether you use a standard measuring cup (225 ml/8 fl oz) or an ordinary teacup to measure the ingredients, because the proportions remain the same.

1 Grease a 1-litre/1¾-pint pudding basin with butter. Sift the flour and mixed spice into a bowl and stir in the sugar, suet and currants, then add the milk and mix well. Spoon the mixture into the prepared basin.

2 Cut out a circle of greaseproof paper and a circle of foil 7.5 cm/3 inches larger than the rim of the basin. Place the paper circle on top of the foil circle, grease it, and pleat both circles across the centre. Place them over the basin, paper-side down, and tie around the rim with string.

3 Place the pudding basin on a trivet in a large saucepan and fill with boiling water to come halfway up the sides. Alternatively, place it in a steamer over a saucepan of boiling water. Steam for 3 hours, then carefully remove from the saucepan. Discard the covering, turn out on to a warmed serving dish and serve with custard.

creamed rice pudding

 cook: 1 hr 5 mins   prep: 5 mins   serves 4

This rich, creamy rice dessert is a really comforting treat on cold winter days. You can serve it with a helping of canned or stewed fruit, or just enjoy it on its own.

NUTRITIONAL INFORMATION

Calories 405

Protein 10g

Carbohydrate 73g

Sugars 42g

Fat 10g

Saturates 6g

INGREDIENTS

140 g/5 oz short-grain rice

1 litre/1¾ pints milk

115 g/4 oz sugar

1 tsp vanilla essence

TO DECORATE

ground cinnamon

cinnamon sticks

variation

For an orange flavour, omit the sugar and vanilla and stir 3 tablespoons of clear honey and the finely grated rind of 1 orange into the milk in Step 1.

1 Rinse the rice well under cold running water and drain. Pour the milk into a large, heavy-based saucepan, add the sugar and bring to the boil, stirring.

2 Add the rice, reduce the heat, cover and simmer gently, stirring occasionally, for 1 hour, or until the milk has been absorbed.

3 Stir in the vanilla essence. Transfer the rice to tall, heatproof glasses, sprinkle with a light dusting of ground cinnamon and serve immediately, decorated with cinnamon sticks.

zabaglione

serves 6 **prep: 5 mins**   **cook: 10 mins**

This light and frothy, warm dessert, which originates from Italy is a welcome treat at the end of a meal. You should serve zabaglione as soon as it is ready, to appreciate its full flavour.

INGREDIENTS

4 egg yolks

70 g/2½ oz caster sugar

125 ml/4 fl oz Marsala wine

amaretti biscuits, to serve

NUTRITIONAL INFORMATION	
Calories 110	
Protein 2g	
Carbohydrate 13g	
Sugars 13g	
Fat 4g	
Saturates 1g	

cook's tip

Decorate the zabaglione with a slit strawberry, placed on the rim of the glass, or serve with sponge fingers or crisp biscuits.

1 Half fill a saucepan with water and bring to the boil. Reduce the heat so that the water is barely simmering. Beat the egg yolks and sugar with an electric whisk until pale and creamy.

2 Set the bowl over the saucepan of water. Do not let the base touch the surface of the water, or the egg yolks will scramble.

3 Gradually add the Marsala wine, beating constantly with the electric whisk. Continue beating until the mixture is thick and has increased in volume. Pour into heatproof glasses or bowls and serve immediately with amaretti biscuits.

flummery

⏱ **cook: 1 hr**   ⏳ **prep: 10 mins, plus 2–3 hrs cooling and chilling**   **serves 4**

This charming, traditional English dessert looks pretty and tastes delicious. It would be a good choice as a cooling dish for a summer dinner party, and should be made well in advance.

NUTRITIONAL INFORMATION	
Calories	544
Protein	. . . . .6g
Carbohydrate	. . . . .45g
Sugars	. . . . .20g
Fat	. . . . .39g
Saturates	. . . . .24g

INGREDIENTS

115 g/4 oz short-grain rice

300 ml/10 fl oz milk

300 ml/10 fl oz double cream, plus

extra for decoration

55 g/2 oz caster sugar

1 tbsp grated lemon rind

1 tsp ground cinnamon, plus

extra for dusting

cook's tip

If you have time, after rinsing the rice, soak it in cold water for 30 minutes, then drain. This helps the grains to absorb the liquid during cooking.

1 Rinse the rice well and place in the top of a double boiler with the milk, cream, sugar, lemon rind and ground cinnamon. Set over a saucepan of gently simmering water, cover and cook, stirring occasionally, for 55 minutes, or until most of the liquid has been absorbed and the rice is tender.

2 Remove the saucepan from the heat and transfer the rice mixture into individual dishes or cups. Leave to cool, then cover and chill in the refrigerator for 2–3 hours, or until set.

3 To serve, whip extra double cream, decorate each dish with a swirl and lightly dust with cinnamon.

syllabub

serves 6   **prep: 10 mins,** ↺ plus chilling (optional)   **cook: 0 mins** ↻

Wine, brandy and cream make this old-fashioned dessert wonderfully self-indulgent – and it is guaranteed to make an impression if you serve it at a dinner party.

INGREDIENTS

175 ml/6 fl oz Madeira

2 tbsp brandy

grated rind of 1 lemon

125 ml/4 fl oz lemon juice

115 g/4 oz caster sugar

600 ml/1 pint double cream

10 amaretti biscuits or ratafias, crumbled

ground cinnamon, to dust

lemon slices, to decorate

NUTRITIONAL INFORMATION	
Calories	.635
Protein	.3g
Carbohydrate	.31g
Sugars	.31g
Fat	.52g
Saturates	.30g

cook's tip

Madeira is a fortified wine from the island of the same name. It may be dry, medium or sweet. Dessert Madeira is best for this recipe – use Bual or Malmsey.

1 Whisk the Madeira, brandy, lemon rind, lemon juice and sugar in a bowl until combined.

2 Add the cream to the bowl and continue whisking until the mixture is thick in consistency.

3 Divide the biscuits between 6 long-stemmed glasses or sundae dishes. Fill each glass or dish with the syllabub mixture and leave in the refrigerator to chill until ready to serve, if desired. Dust the surface of each dessert with cinnamon and decorate with lemon slices.

flambéed peaches

 cook: 5 mins   prep: 5 mins   serves 4

This dessert is a fabulous end to a dinner party – especially if your guests are watching you cook. It makes a luxurious but, at the same time, refreshing final course.

NUTRITIONAL INFORMATION

Calories 227

Protein 3g

Carbohydrate 26g

Sugars 26g

Fat 11g

Saturates 6g

INGREDIENTS

3 tbsp unsalted butter

3 tbsp muscovado sugar

4 tbsp orange juice

4 peaches, peeled, halved and stoned

2 tbsp almond liqueur or

peach brandy

4 tbsp toasted flaked almonds

cook's tip

Igniting the spirit will burn off the alcohol and mellow the flavour. However, if you are serving this dessert to children, you can omit the almond liqueur or brandy.

1 Heat the butter, muscovado sugar and orange juice in a large, heavy-based frying pan over a low heat, stirring constantly, until the butter has melted and the sugar has dissolved.

2 Add the peaches and cook for 1–2 minutes on each side, or until golden.

3 Add the almond liqueur and ignite with a match or taper. When the flames have died down, transfer to serving dishes, sprinkle with toasted flaked almonds and serve immediately.

warm fruit compote

serves 4   prep: 10 mins ⟲   cook: 8-10 mins ⏲

A bowl of warm summer fruits suffused with exotic spices releases a burst of flavours on to the palate. The velvety syrup is sure to make this fresh, sumptuous dish a firm favourite.

INGREDIENTS

4 plums, halved and stoned

225 g/8 oz raspberries

225 g/8 oz strawberries,
hulled and halved

2 tbsp muscovado sugar

2 tbsp dry white wine

2 star anise

4 cloves

1 cinnamon stick

NUTRITIONAL INFORMATION

Calories 95

Protein 2g

Carbohydrate 21g

Sugars 21g

Fat 0g

Saturates 0g

1 Place all the ingredients in a large heavy-based saucepan. Cook over a low heat, stirring occasionally, until the sugar has dissolved.

2 Cover tightly and simmer very gently for 5 minutes, or until the fruit is tender but still retains its shape. Do not let the mixture boil.

3 Remove and discard the star anise, cloves and cinnamon, and serve the compote warm.

cook's tip

These lightly cooked summer fruits will taste their best if you serve them with a helping of fresh single cream or plain vanilla ice cream.

clafoutis

cook: 45 mins   **prep: 15 mins,**   serves 4
                            plus 1 hr standing

Although the many different recipes for this unusual, batter-based dessert may use a variety of fruits, cherries are the classic filling in Limousin in France, where the dish originated.

NUTRITIONAL INFORMATION

Calories 297

Protein 7g

Carbohydrate 42g

Sugars 31g

Fat 11g

Saturates 6g

INGREDIENTS

450 g/1 lb sweet black cherries

2 tbsp cherry brandy

1 tbsp icing sugar, plus

extra for dusting

butter, for greasing

BATTER

3 tbsp plain flour

3 tbsp sugar

175 ml/6 fl oz single cream

2 eggs, lightly beaten

grated rind of ½ lemon

¼ tsp vanilla essence

cook's tip

Traditionally, in Limousin, the cherries are not stoned before cooking, because the stones are thought to release extra flavour into the dessert.

1 Preheat the oven to 190°C/375°F/Gas Mark 5. Stone the cherries, then place in a bowl with the cherry brandy and icing sugar and mix together. Cover with clingfilm and leave to stand for 1 hour.

2 Meanwhile, grease a shallow, ovenproof dish with butter. To make the batter, sift the flour into a bowl and stir in the sugar. Gradually whisk in the single cream, beaten eggs, lemon rind and vanilla essence. Whisk constantly until the batter is completely smooth.

3 Spoon the cherries into the ovenproof dish and pour the batter over them to cover. Bake in the preheated oven for 45 minutes, or until golden and set. Lightly dust with extra icing sugar and serve warm, or leave to cool to room temperature before serving.

pancake pieces

cook: 10 mins   **prep: 15 mins**   serves 4

variation

These pancake pieces are also delicious mixed with 400 g/14 oz of canned morello cherries in syrup, instead of the apricots.

This is a cheap and cheerful, easy-to-make dessert that is perfect for midweek family suppers, and surprisingly filling. Its casual presentation makes it a favourite with children.

INGREDIENTS

2 tbsp caster sugar

1 tsp ground cinnamon

125 g/4½ oz plain flour

pinch of salt

2 eggs, lightly beaten

125 ml/4 fl oz milk

400 g/14 oz canned apricot halves in syrup

sunflower oil, for brushing

cook's tip

Before you add the batter to the frying pan, make sure the oil is very hot. Tilt and roll the frying pan as you pour the batter in, to spread it over the base in a thin layer.

1 Place the sugar and cinnamon in a bowl, stir to mix and reserve. Sift the flour and salt into a separate bowl. Whisk the eggs and milk into the flour and continue whisking to make a smooth batter.

2 Drain the apricot halves, reserving the syrup, then whisk the syrup into the batter until combined. Roughly chop the apricots and reserve.

3 Heat a large crêpe pan or heavy-based frying pan and brush with oil. Pour in the batter and cook over a medium heat for 4–5 minutes, or until the underside is golden brown. Turn over with a fish slice or palette knife and cook the second side for 4 minutes, or until golden. Tear the pancake into bite-sized pieces with 2 spoons or forks.

4 Add the apricots to the pan and heat through briefly. Divide the pancake pieces and apricots between individual plates, sprinkle with the sugar and cinnamon mixture and serve immediately.

caramelised oranges

serves 6

prep: 25 mins, plus 1–2 hrs chilling

cook: 15–20 mins

These unusual, sugar-coated oranges look almost too pretty to eat – but make sure you do, because they taste wonderfully refreshing, with a real citrus tang.

INGREDIENTS

6 large oranges

5 tbsp water

100 g/3½ oz caster sugar

whipped cream, to serve

NUTRITIONAL INFORMATION

Calories	.143
Protein	.2g
Carbohydrate	.35g
Sugars	.35g
Fat	.0g
Saturates	.0g

cook's tip

For recipes using citrus peel, look for unwaxed specimens – that is, those that have not been treated with diphenyl to preserve their colour.

1 Carefully pare wide strips of rind from 2 of the oranges using a swivel-blade vegetable peeler. Cut the strips of rind into thin batons with a sharp knife and reserve a few for decoration. Peel all the oranges and remove traces of white pith. Cut the fruit horizontally into slices 1-cm/½-inch thick. Place in a serving bowl and tip in any spilt juice.

2 Before making the caramel, half-fill the sink with cold water. Place 3 tablespoons of water and all of the sugar in a heavy-based saucepan and bring to the boil, stirring constantly, until the sugar has dissolved. Boil, without stirring, until the syrup is a dark caramel colour. Remove the saucepan from the heat and carefully immerse the

base in the cold water to prevent any further cooking.

3 Add the remaining 2 tablespoons of water to the saucepan with the orange rind and simmer over a low heat, stirring occasionally, for 8–10 minutes, or until the rind is almost translucent. Pour the mixture over the orange slices, turning them to coat.

Cool completely, then chill in the refrigerator for 1–2 hours. Serve with whipped cream, decorated with orange rind.

forest fruits granita

⏲ **cook: 5 mins**   ⏱ **prep: 15 mins, plus 3–4 hrs cooling and freezing**   **serves 4**

This is the perfect dessert for a hot summer's day. It's more cooling and less calorie-packed than ice cream, but is packed with a great combination of fruity flavours.

NUTRITIONAL INFORMATION

Calories 175

Protein 2g

Carbohydrate 44g

Sugars 44g

Fat 0g

Saturates 0g

INGREDIENTS

225 g/8 oz strawberries, hulled

175 g/6 oz raspberries

175 g/6 oz blackberries, plus extra

to decorate

1–2 tbsp lemon juice (optional)

140 g/5 oz caster sugar

150 ml/5 fl oz water

TO DECORATE

whipped cream

fresh mint sprigs

variation

For a really lazy granita, replace the fruit purée with 1 litre/1¾ pints of fruit juice, such as orange or cranberry juice.

1 Place the strawberries, raspberries and blackberries in a blender or food processor and process to a purée. Push the purée through a fine-meshed sieve into a freezerproof container to remove the seeds. Add lemon juice to taste.

2 Place the caster sugar and water in a small saucepan over a low heat and stir until the sugar has dissolved. Pour the syrup over the fruit purée and stir well to combine. Leave to cool, stirring occasionally, then cover and place in the freezer for 2–3 hours, or until set.

3 Transfer the frozen granita mixture into the refrigerator 30 minutes before serving. Spoon into tall glasses or glass cups, decorate with whipped cream, blackberries and fresh mint sprigs. Serve.

blueberry compote

serves 6

prep: 10 mins, ↻
plus 2–3 hrs chilling

cook: 5 mins ⏲

Serve this easy and attractive dish with whipped cream or ice cream and small, sweet, dessert biscuits. It is perfect for entertaining, as it has to be made in advance and chilled.

INGREDIENTS

675 g/1 lb 8 oz blueberries

280 g/10 oz caster sugar

1 tbsp water

2 tbsp gin

dessert biscuits, to serve

NUTRITIONAL INFORMATION

Calories 229

Protein 1g

Carbohydrate 57g

Sugars 57g

Fat 0g

Saturates 0g

variation

You can substitute fresh redcurrants for the blueberries and brandy for the gin, if you prefer.

1 Place the blueberries, sugar and water in a heavy-based saucepan over a low heat, shaking the saucepan occasionally, until the sugar has dissolved.

2 Remove the saucepan from the heat and gradually stir in the gin, then leave the mixture to cool completely.

3 Transfer the compote to dishes, cover and leave to chill in the refrigerator for 2–3 hours before serving with dessert biscuits.

apple fritters

⏱ **cook: 4–6 mins** 🕑 **prep: 15 mins,
plus 30 mins standing** **serves 4**

*This is a very popular choice for family meals, as children and adults
alike love the flavour and crispy texture of the apple rings – and you
don't need a spoon or fork to eat them.*

NUTRITIONAL INFORMATION	
Calories	.437
Protein	.7g
Carbohydrate	.35g
Sugars	.14g
Fat	.31g
Saturates	.18g

INGREDIENTS

115 g/4 oz plain flour

pinch of salt

2 egg yolks

1 egg white

1 tbsp sunflower oil

150 ml/5 fl oz milk

450 g/1 lb cooking apples

juice of 1 lemon

caster sugar, for sprinkling

115 g/4 oz unsalted butter

crème fraîche, to serve

cook's tip

Choose firm, tart apples for
this dish, such as Bramleys or
Granny Smith's. Once they are
cut, they should be sprinkled
with lemon juice immediately
and cooked quickly to prevent
any discoloration.

1 Sift the flour and salt
into a mixing bowl.
Make a well in the centre
and add the egg yolks, egg
white and oil. Gradually
incorporate the flour into the
liquid with a wooden spoon.
Gradually beat in the milk and
continue beating to make a
smooth batter. Cover with
clingfilm and leave to stand for
30 minutes.

2 Peel and core the
apples, then cut them
into rings about 5-mm/¼-inch
thick. Spread them out on a
plate and sprinkle with the
lemon juice and caster sugar.

3 Melt the butter in a
large, heavy-based
frying pan over a medium
heat. Dip the apple rings into
the batter, one at a time, then

drop them into the frying pan.
Cook for 2–3 minutes on each
side, or until golden. Transfer
to a serving platter, sprinkle
with more caster sugar and
serve with crème fraîche.

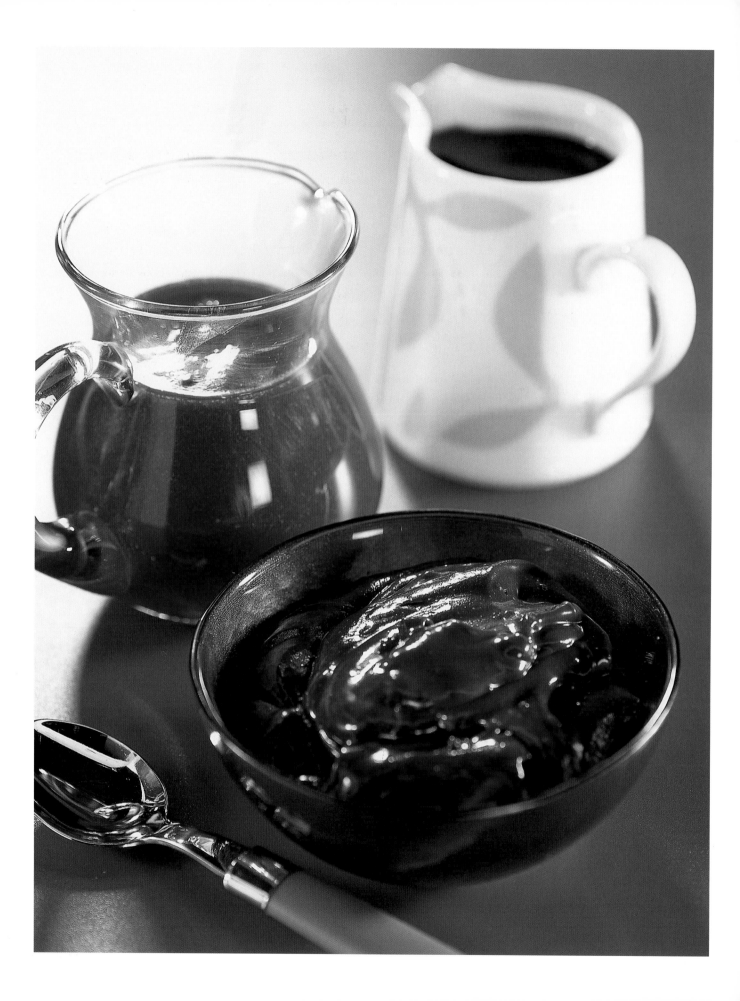

saucy ice creams

cook: 5–10 mins

prep: 5–10 mins, plus 1 hr cooling and chilling

serves 6

Ice cream is a great freezer standby for dessert, but it can be a little dull and uninspiring. The best way to liven it up is to serve it with a selection of tasty, syrupy sauces.

INGREDIENTS

BERRY SAUCE

225 g/8 oz berries, such as blackberries or raspberries

2 tbsp water

2–3 tbsp caster sugar

2 tbsp fruit liqueur, such as crème de cassis or crème de framboise

CHOCOLATE SAUCE

150 ml/5 fl oz double cream

55 g/2 oz unsalted butter

55 g/2 oz light muscovado sugar

175 g/6 oz plain chocolate, broken into pieces

2 tbsp rum (optional)

PORT SAUCE

350 ml/12 fl oz ruby port

2 tsp cornflour

variation

You can substitute other fruit, such as pineapple rings or apricots for the apples, if you prefer.

cook's tip

All of the sauces taste spectacular served with plain vanilla ice cream, but ring the changes and try out lots of combinations to find out which sauce you prefer with your favourite flavoured ice cream.

1 To make the berry sauce, place all the ingredients in a saucepan over a low heat, stirring occasionally, until the sugar has dissolved and the fruit juices run. Purée with a hand-held blender or in a food processor, then push through a sieve into a bowl to remove the seeds. Add more sugar, if necessary. Serve warm or cold.

2 To make the chocolate sauce, pour the cream into the top of a double boiler and add the butter and sugar. Set over a saucepan of barely simmering water and stir until smooth. Remove from the heat, leave to cool slightly, then add the chocolate, stirring until melted. Stir in the rum (if using). Leave to cool to room temperature before serving.

3 To make the port sauce, place 50 ml/ 2 fl oz of the port in a bowl with the cornflour and stir to make a smooth paste. Pour the remainder of the port into a saucepan and bring to the boil. Stir in the cornflour paste and cook over a high heat, stirring, for 1 minute, or until thickened. Remove the sauce from the heat and leave to cool. Pour into a bowl, cover and chill in the refrigerator for 30 minutes before serving.

index

index